ROOM FULL OF REFERRALS®

..."and how to network for them!"

Dr. Tony Alessandra
Dr. Ivan Misner
Dawn Lyons

Room Full of Referrals®
...and How to Network For Them

To contact Referral Institute:
www.referralinstitute.com
office@referralinstitute.com

A Paradigm Publishing Book

ISBN 978-0-9740819-8-4

— Credits —

Editor: Jason Holland, Profit Boosting Copy

Cover and Inside Book Design by Douglas Silva
Midnite Graphics

Printed in the USA

To the tens of thousands of Referral Institute clients
and BNI members around the globe who truly see
the value in honoring others by behavioral style,
we dedicate this book to you! Help us change
how business relationships are developed!

We thank our families for their encouragement,
support and, most importantly, for always
believing in us.

Live in your Style!
Dawn Lyons

CONTENTS

Why We Wrote this Book

Our qualifications and why the three of us decided to write Room Full of Referrals® will play a huge role in your understanding our viewpoint throughout the entire book. So, we'd like tell you a little bit about ourselves and our motivations for sharing our knowledge of behavioral styles and referral marketing. You'll find complete biographies at the back of the book.

Dr. Tony Alessandra has a street-wise, college-smart perspective on business, having been raised in the housing projects of New York City to eventually realizing success as a graduate professor of marketing, entrepreneur, business author, and hall-of-fame keynote speaker.

Dr. Alessandra is a prolific author on the subjects of business, networking, selling, and more, with 27 books translated into over 50 foreign language editions. He is also the originator of the internationally-recognized behavioral style assessment tool: the Platinum Rule®.

Dr. Ivan Misner, having used behavioral styles extensively during his time as a business consultant to help companies thrive and motivate their employees, is still implementing this material in his businesses 30 years later.

As Senior Partner of the Referral Institute he oversees the teaching of this material in 13 different countries. Dr. Misner is the founder and chairman of BNI (www.bni.com), the world's largest business networking organization, and Senior Partner of the Referral Institute. BNI was founded in 1985. The organization has almost 6,200 chapters throughout every populated continent of the world. Last year alone, BNI generated 6.9 million referrals resulting in $3.1 billion dollars' worth of business for its members.

Called the "Father of Modern Networking" by CNN and the "Networking Guru" by Entrepreneur magazine, Dr. Misner is considered one of the world's leading experts on business networking and has been a keynote speaker for major corporations and associations throughout the world.

Dawn Lyons has spent over 24+ years learning, understanding and applying behavioral styles into her life. It was in December of 1988 that Dawn was exposed to a seminar that gave a very short description about the different behavioral styles. Realizing at 18 years old how important this information could be, she set out to master the material. Since then, Dawn has been hired to speak in Ireland, Germany, the United Kingdom, Australia, Sweden and all across the U.S. to audiences of 500+.

Dawn's expertise lies in being able to identify the different styles and immediately adapt pace of speech, eye contact, posture, hand gestures and even language.

So what do the three of us have in common? Well, in total we have more than 90 years of expertise in behavioral styles. We have more than 80 years of working with business owners. Trust us, we have seen the good, the bad and the ugly.

Ivan and Dawn are business partners in the Referral Institute, and Dawn is a top-producing BNI franchise owner. Ivan's extensive network led to an introduction to Tony, and now the Referral Institute uses Tony's Platinum Rule® Assessment to help Referral Institute clients understand how their behavioral style is affecting their referability!

We've combined our experience to give you documented, proven information to help you understand where you are right now with your expertise in referral marketing and behavioral styles, and how far you can truly advance with it using the knowledge in this book. Let's get started!

Why You Want to Read this Book
By Dawn Lyons

Have you ever walked into a room full of people and thought, "How can I get referrals from this group?" I am sure you have! As business owners we walk into rooms full of people all the time. And we recognize these as ideal opportunities for generating referrals.

But if you don't know how to effectively gain referrals in these situations, the opportunity is lost.

As an entrepreneur referrals are a major way of generating new business. Yet in virtually all of the Referral Institute seminars I have taught around the world, when I ask the audience, "Who in this room is getting all of the referrals they want?" No one raises a hand! It's as if referrals are these magical, wonderful pieces of new business that just seem to appear now and again. They have no idea how to re-create the scenario that led to their appearance often enough to make them happy with their referral revenue.

The majority of business owners I speak to do not even have a specific dollar amount or percentage of their overall revenue that they would like to obtain by referral. It's amazing. So many people talk about wanting more referrals but have absolutely no plan for how to get them.

Are you frustrated with the amount of referrals you are receiving for your business?

Do you feel that more people could be generating referrals for you but are simply not doing it? Are you convinced that your business would run smoother and you would have better quality clients if you could just gain a steady flow of referrals?

There is a solution. It's a philosophy I passionately believe in. If you choose to adopt it, I am convinced you can bring in all the referrals you need for your business to absolutely thrive!

Please read the following phrase very slowly so you understand the true depth of this statement.

People know people, and the people people know, know more people. So, if referrals come from people, who should we be learning more about? People!

Yes, you got it!

Simon Sinek, the author of *Start with Why*, is known for teaching leaders how to inspire people to action. One of his quotes that we love, and that fully relates to what we are talking about here, is: "If you don't understand people, you don't understand business."

Think about it. In referral marketing, those targeted clients you want are people. The referral sources you want to give you more business are people. The vendors you work with… are people! As an entrepreneur, you cannot get away from people in your business; they're all around you!

This book is titled *Room Full of Referrals®* for a reason. When you attend networking functions you are aware that every time you walk into a room full of people, it's the ideal place to generate referrals for those people and receive referrals from them. So isn't it true that you are actually walking into a Room Full of Referrals®? It's a different perspective, isn't it? If you truly realized that you were walking into a Room Full of Referrals® you would have a different intention, select different topics of conversation, approach people differently, etc.

Knowing how to network for referrals is the key thing here. And you must keep in mind that as you network your behavioral style can help you or hinder you.

So how should you act? How can you elevate your professional image and appeal to all of the styles? To quote one of the "founding fathers" of behavioral styles and the inventor of the DiSC® assessment, Dr. William Moulton Marston: "People exhibit all four styles in varying degrees of intensity." These different levels of intensity make you who you are.

So, if you are in a Room Full of Referrals® how can you identify and react appropriately to the behavioral styles of others and have your behavioral style attract them to you versus turn them off?

In referral marketing, there is something called your "referability." When others find it easy and enjoyable to refer prospects to your business, your referability level is probably high. If others are unwilling or find it difficult to refer new business to you, your referability level may be very low.

In most cases, if others consider you an expert in your profession, believe you will treat their prospects appropriately, and truly want to help you succeed, then they will be inspired to generate referrals on your behalf. They will do it often and with ease. This is your level of referability! The more referrals you are receiving from all of your sources, the more referable you are!

What you must realize is this: Your behavioral style IS affecting your referability! I came to this realization more than six years ago, and I insist that every one of my Referral Institute clients be aware of this fact as it affects every aspect of their referral marketing plan.

Your behavioral style IS affecting your referability!

This book will help you understand your own behavioral style and how it is affecting your referability. You'll also learn how to identify behavioral styles in others and, most importantly, learn how to adapt your own approach to those different styles.

Referral marketing leads to few – if any – overnight success stories. In fact, the most crucial part is building relationships, which takes a lot of time and effort. However, when you've taken the time to build the right referral relationships with the right people, and you are able to understand each of their behavioral styles, these long-term relationships will be a huge part of your referral marketing business.

Let me give you an example:

Imagine you're at a networking function, and you meet someone who's in a profession that could refer you very easily. You're enjoying your conversation, and you feel that this could be a good connection. So, you decide to set up a lunch meeting.

At lunch, the person starts asking a lot of detailed questions. He wants to know how long you've been in business, what your company organization looks like, your whole list of products and services, how much you charge for these services, etc. He asks all sorts of technical questions, too.

For those in one particular behavioral style it would be hard for them to understand why in the world he would want all this information. For them, this type of questioning almost seems suspicious for a "get to know you better" meeting.

But for the questioner, who has a different behavioral style, it's completely natural. They feel they need this type of information before making a referral.

Can you see how the two styles did what was natural for them? One wanted to gather all of the information possible. The other just wanted to hang out and get to know each other at a very surface level. One felt he was getting necessary information. The other felt like it was an interrogation. As a result both sides walk away feeling awkward and exhausted.

Please understand neither person was right or wrong. It's simply how people are wired. There are some who need all of the information and all of the details in order to move forward in a relationship. Others take their time in getting to know you and really build the relationship before looking for all of that data. They want to know you as a person first, then as a business person.

Here's the issue: The person needing all of the information could be someone who can generate consistent referrals for you over the long-term. However, if you don't understand the behavioral style up front and don't know how to work with them, you could decide not to develop the relationship. This could be a big mistake.

Have I grabbed your attention so far? Are you wondering how many referral opportunities you might have missed by not communicating well with someone who has a different "style" than you do?

Read on! This book will give you tons of answers and insights into how your behavioral style IS affecting your referability and give you comprehensive strategies for turning things around.

CHAPTER 1
Becoming Aware of Behavioral Styles

A Story from Dawn: Facing Off with the "Big" Man

I'm at our Referral Institute training center in Petaluma, California, about to present our Referral Success 101 program. This session is special as I'm anticipating a specific person to be there – someone who was referred to me.

I want to make a good impression, of course, so I'm really focused on understanding his behavioral style right off the bat so I can speak to him in "his" language. I really want to get this right. I am an expert at this for crying out loud!

As I fiddle with some papers and make small talk with the first couple of people to arrive, it happens. He walks through the door, and I am "on."

He lumbers toward me with gigantic steps, clad in clean brown work boots, blue jeans, and button-down logo'd shirt. He has to be 6'3". As he begins to speak from more than 30 feet away his voice resonates through the entire place, and I know immediately he is a force to be reckoned with.

"Hi, I am Ron Smith," he bellows. "You must be Dawn Lyons. I was told to ask for you. Bob referred me. He says you are the best at this and that I needed to be here!"

I rise from my seat, stand as tall as I possibly can (thank God for 3-inch heels), and brace myself for impact. The handshake is excruciating and exciting at the same time. I take a deep breath and fight the urge to show any sign of pain in my crushed hand.

"Well, hello Ron Smith. I AM Dawn Lyons. I AM the person you are to meet. I am VERY good at this, and yes, Bob told me you would be here!" I reply in my most confident voice with perfect eye contact, exuding complete control and competence.

Whew, I think I did it. I met him where he was at but did not over step my bounds, did not say anything too wimpy or too nice. I just answered his pace and intensity and let him know I can handle his "big" stature. I already like his energy. Now I need to make sure I engage in the right conversation in order to let him know that wherever he wants to take his company, I can help.

I already know several things that are affecting his referability, and I've only spent 20 seconds with him. Wow, I think to myself, does he even know? It seems so simple to me… will he be able to see it?

Meanwhile the other people in the room are making small talk, getting water and signing in. I smile at a lady that has on a fuchsia-colored jacket with a neon green camisole underneath, sporting a watch that has sparkles around the entire band, and no they are not diamonds. In a later chapter, you will understand which of the four behavioral styles this lady is, and why I included the sentence here!

Then I tell Ron that I need to welcome the rest of the folks coming in. But before I leave, I ask him my favorite question: "So, how is business really going for you?"

I get the standard, "Well, with the economy... " that I've heard so many times. When he finishes, I ask my next favorite question: "So, I have to wonder, is there someone in your industry who will earn seven figures this year?"

"Yes, I am sure someone will," he replies.

"In this area?" I press.

He says yeah with a shrug of his shoulders as if he doesn't care. But it takes him by surprise when I counter with this: "Well then, all we have to figure out is… why isn't that business coming to you!?"

He steps back slightly, pondering the statement, and says, "Well, if you can do that, then you are hired!"

Ah yes, music to my ears!

"We can absolutely make that happen," I continue. "But how about we start with the basics, Referral Success 101, and take it from there?"

He agrees, and I go mingle with the others, knowing I accomplished several things with Ron. I...

- Exuded confidence
- Met his pace and intensity
- Let him know I am an expert and can help him
- Got him thinking about what he wants, and why it's not coming to him by referral
- Got him to want to hire me already, and he hasn't even heard me speak
- Gave him a bit of a takeaway as he has lots to learn about referrals
- Gave him hope that there is a way to get his business to be more successful

"Not bad for a 90 second conversation," I say to myself.

The Key to Effective Interaction with People

This is a perfect example of becoming aware of behavioral styles. If you really have a passion for understanding others, you will want to learn and understand as much as you can about people you encounter. Becoming aware of behavioral styles can really change how you will interact with each and every person you meet, depending, of course, how serious you are about this information.

Dawn had a choice in the above story. She could have not utilized her behavioral style knowledge and brought her own style to the conversation and hoped for the best. Instead she chose to use her knowledge and adapt accordingly to make the encounter that much better for Ron. In this book, you will gain a thorough understanding of behavioral styles and how to adapt yourself to situations and encounters just as Dawn did. And after lots of practice, it will become second nature.

Our number one intention is to make sure that we honor and respect each and every person that we come in contact with and adapt our style to theirs so they have a fantastic engagement with us. Keep in mind that in the process of gathering information about a person's behavioral style, the best anyone can make is an educated guess.

You may not always get it exactly right. But we do know that if you can identify the top two behavioral styles of people that you meet and can use that information to speak to them in their language, then they are going to be very comfortable continuing the conversation with you and may even open up very quickly.

The Art of Diplomacy

By Ivan Misner

> I was asked at an event once to share the best piece of advice I had ever gotten.
>
> It was an easy answer. It was from my mother when I was running for student government in high school.
>
> She said, "Honey, you're not going to get elected dog-catcher unless you learn how to work better with people."
>
> She gave me a paperweight, which you'll still find on the desk in my home office to this day, which says:
>
> "Diplomacy is the art of letting someone else have your way."
>
> It means that you have to work with people, not through people.

We understand that when first learning behavioral styles it can be really difficult. In a matter of seconds, we are convincing our brain to acquire and decipher an incredible amount of information while looking and acting like a normal person.

Here is our top 13 list of what you should be listening or watching for when you meet new people. Remember the description of Ron!

Behavioral Style Indicators

1. Pace

Listen to the pace of their speech. Is it fast or slow? Are you struggling to keep up with them or are you bored and losing interest? Do you find yourself finishing their sentences because they aren't speaking fast enough? Watch the way they walk. Are they "making a beeline" for something? Or are they just moseying around, taking their time?

2. Tasks vs. People

As you begin talking to them, do they tend to be focused on task-oriented or people-oriented items? You will notice very little "emotional" dialogue with task-oriented folks, and they focus on "what and how." Those who are people-oriented will share much more with you and focus on the "who."

A Story from Tony: An Extremely Task-Oriented Friend

The first time my friend Dennis called my home and my wife answered, he simply said, "Tony," in a gruff voice. That's it.

She hands me the phone. It's a short call. And when I hang up, she asks me, "Who was that?"

"My friend Dennis," I tell her.

"I have to tell you," she says. "That guy has zero social skills. Unbelievable how rude he is."

I explain that's how Dennis is. He's got a lot of positives, but that's one of his shortcomings. Then she says that's a real problem for *me*.

"You teach communication skills and relationship building, and you have a friend like this," she explains. "What does it say to the world about your techniques?"

I tell you, that was right between the eyes.

She encouraged me to take him under my wing to show people how effective my teaching was.

So I did 90 days of personal coaching with Dennis to help him communicate with others that weren't as task-oriented and perceived his behavioral style as rude. And it was one of the most dramatic turnarounds in a person's behavior I've ever seen.

In 90 short days, he would call my house and say, "Sue? Dennis. Tony." That's 300% improvement. You don't get a lot better than that!

But seriously, Dennis did turn things around, and today he's a much better communicator.

---

3. Clothing

You can learn a lot about people by what they wear. Do they have "loud" clothing with prints or patterns? Are they dressed professionally or casually... in flashy colors (like the fuchsia jacket and neon green camisole)... or pastels? Do their clothes look comfortable, tight-fitting, trendy or dated? "Label dropping" can also reveal much. Maybe you say, "I like your suit," and they reply, "Thanks, it's an Armani."

Also, wearing logo'd attire says they aren't afraid to promote themselves and make their brand visible. Men in the professional world reveal information with their ties. There's the simple solid color tie, the "power" tie, the loud and flashy tie, as well as those with little pictures and decorations and even some with "save the [insert animal here]."

4. Jewelry and Accessories

Are they wearing all silver, all gold, or mixed? Do they have on flashy, sparkly rhinestones or a large, single diamond? Does their jewelry appear to have sentimental value? Are they wearing just a simple wedding band? Many people have also started to accessorize with glasses or colored contacts.

5. Makeup

How much makeup are they wearing… or are they wearing any at all? Do they look totally "made up" or natural? Are they wearing a bold lip color or simply a subtle lip gloss?

6. Shoes

Are they fashionably trendy or wearing comfortable shoes? Stilettos or flats? Polished or not? Brand name or not? Also, the condition of the shoes – regardless of style – is very important. Remember the clean work boots that Ron had on?

7. Facial Expressions

Are they serious or excitable? Do they smile often or have a "poker face"? Do they exaggerate their expressions or are they stoic? Do they give winks, raise their eyebrows dramatically or crinkle their noses?

8. Gestures

Do they talk with their hands? Are they "touchy feely"? Are their gestures closer to the body or more open and further away from the body? Are they reserved or outgoing with their gestures? Do they touch your shoulder or arm when first meeting you? Gestures can also have a pace to them; are they fast or slow?

9. Body Language

Is their body language open or closed? Do they seem approachable and easygoing or hard to get to know and standoffish? Are their arms often crossed in front of their chest? Do they tend to lean into or away from you? Is their weight shifted to the back and on one foot or do they seem firmly planted in one spot?

10. Eye Contact

Do they give you direct eye contact or look down frequently? Do they often look away at who may be coming into the room while speaking with you? Once you have eye contact, do they disengage first or often?

11. Handshake

A person's handshake tells you a lot about their style. Is it firm? Double-clasped? Limp? A very excited quadruple-pump? Does it feel controlling, where they might turn your hand as they grab it, or do they shake it so fast you can tell they don't want to be touching you at all? Also, what they say as you are shaking hands is very important. Do they introduce themselves with first and last name? Do they not even tell you their first name?

12. Verbiage

Are their words fun, exciting and outgoing or more reserved, controlled and soft-spoken? Are they direct and to the point or very detailed and process-oriented? Do they tend to ask a lot of questions before being able to move forward, or do they say something like, "Okay, whatever, we can figure it out later"?

13. Cars

As you are arriving or leaving a meeting, you may notice their car. Look to see if it's sensible and non-flashy, name brand and expensive, older, a hybrid or fun and fast – especially a convertible.

All of this information is going through our brains as we meet someone for the first time, trying to identify what style they are. It's a lot of information to process, but we promise it can become second nature – if you are willing to practice.

There are a few key points to take into consideration:

1) You can learn this knowledge and apply it only to yourself.
2) You can learn this knowledge and understand yourself, plus use it with others when or if you think about it.
3) You can learn this knowledge, understand yourself and how you affect others, use it to benefit others as you interact with them, and implement it as a daily habit to develop incredible long-term relationships.

What we see for most people is that they don't follow through on every aspect of what we are about to explain and rarely achieve number three above. They simply gain the knowledge and apply it to themselves... and then wonder why they're not getting the right results. Our hope is that you become a K.I.D. with this information.

A K.I.D. is a person who...

Has the *Knowledge* and can follow through on the *Implementation* of that knowledge to *Develop* habits and relationships.

If you truly take the time to learn and internalize this knowledge and then implement it into your daily activities, we believe you can create the right relationships and have the referral marketing success you are looking for! Besides, couldn't we all spend a bit more time acting like a K.I.D.?

CHAPTER 2
The Science Behind Behavioral Styles

People have been both frustrated and fascinated with each other's differences for thousands of years. The earliest recorded efforts to explain our differences were made by astrologers who recorded the positions of the heavens. The 12 signs in four basic groupings - Earth, Air, Fire, and Water - are still used today.

In ancient Greece, Hippocrates' concept of four temperaments followed: Sanguine, Phlegmatic, Melancholy and Choleric. He viewed personality as shaped by blood, phlegm, black bile and yellow bile. As unpalatable as this might sound to us, people accepted these physical or bodily causes for varying "humours" for centuries.

Respected figures from medical/physical sciences, metaphysics, mathematics and philosophy observed these four temperaments, including Aristotle, Empedocles, Theophrastus and, in Roman times, Galen. References to Hippocrates' Big Four can be found in Shakespeare's plays.

We still use these terms, especially in the SAT college admissions test and in reference to babies and young children. "Jason looks so serious and melancholy for a one-year-old," or "Jennifer has a sanguine, ruddy-faced disposition."

In 1923, Dr. Carl Jung wrote his famous Psychological Types, at that time the most sophisticated scientific work on personality. In it, he again described four behavioral styles: Intuitor, Thinker, Feeler and Sensor.

This basic, four-type model spans all cultures, East and West, north and south. For instance, contemporary Japan still studies behavior and physical composition. *Advice on How to Form a Good Combination of Blood Types*, a best seller by Toshitaka Nomi, claimed 100,000 documented cases of cross-referencing personalities with blood types. Nomi indicated that 40 percent of Japan's population has Type A blood.

He associated this with the conscientious, hard-working behavior expected of engineers and technicians. He hypothesized that this explained Japan's emphasis on high-technology excellence.

The modern take on behavior profiles was conceived and written about by psychologist William Moulton Marston in 1928. Behavior profiles undergone many transformations since then, with the most important transformations in the tools used to measure people according to Marston's original model.

In his book, *Emotions of Normal People*, Marston exhibited his keen interest in the ways a person's emotions can affect or be visible in physical symptoms or expressions. He categorized emotional expression into the following types:

- Dominance (D)
- Inducement (I)
- Submission (S)
- Compliance (C)

He placed these types into a two-axis model that was divided by these dimensions: Perception of the environment, or seeing it as favorable or unfavorable; and perception of one's power *within* that environment, a measure of whether one feels more – or less – powerful than this environment.

After combining the two dimensions, Marston was able to summarize the model as follows*:

1. **Dominance:** Perceiving oneself as more powerful than the environment and believes the environment is unfavorable.
2. **Inducement:** Perceiving oneself as more powerful than the environment and perceives the environment as favorable.
3. **Submission:** Perceiving oneself as less powerful than the environment and perceives the environment as favorable.
4. **Compliance:** Perceiving oneself as more powerful than the environment and perceives the environment as unfavorable.

**The DiSC® Indra® Research Report, Pamela Cole & Kathleen Tuzinski*

With all the interest that Marston's model gained, it became apparent it needed an instrument to measure it. In the 1940s, other professionals came forward to do just this – while still adhering to Marston's original model and paradigm.

In his efforts to create a test to aid in employee selection, industrial psychologist Walter V. Clarke came up with several adjectives, allowing potential employees to check off the ones that they felt described them. Interestingly, four distinct areas of personality/behavioral style emerged:

- Aggressive
- Sociable
- Stable
- Avoidant

When analyzing these areas, Clarke realized that, in effect, they mirrored the model developed by Marston just over a decade earlier. With that realization, even though it wasn't what he originally intended to do, Clarke was able to create a complex instrument that was able to measure people based on Marston's original model. This model became to be known as DiSC® profiles.

In the early '50s, John P. Cleaver, an engineer who felt that "modern businesses had lost sight of the inherent human factor in jobs," decided to pursue his belief that each employee should be measured and evaluated for compatibility with their role in the organization."[2]

He enlisted the services of staff at Walter Clarke Associates and collaborated with them to fine-tune Clarke's original measuring instrument into a tool called the Self Description method. It was able to decrease the occurrences of "socially-desirable responding" – in effect, Cleaver's user-friendly, self-description assessment made the DiSC® model much easier to understand. Today, almost every DiSC® system in use today is a variation of the Cleaver material.

Studies on over 7,000 people worldwide, with a wide demographic range, have proven the validity of Marston's original DiSC® model, as well as the Cleaver assessment and its subsequent variations.

What we are doing in this book is using the core concepts found in DiSC®. However, we are evaluating them specifically in how they relate to one's referability.

A note from Ivan: Interestingly, I'm just a few degrees of separation from Marston. After joining his firm J.P. Cleaver as a consultant, I was trained in DiSC® by an expert who was trained by J.P. Cleaver himself.

[2] *CleaverCompany.com*

CHAPTER 3
Who Are You?

It's a simple question, with a ton of potential answers: Who are you?

You might be a dad, a mom, a brother, a sister, a teacher, a lawyer, an entrepreneur, a sports fan, a music lover, a world traveler... you might be one or many things. But who *are* you, really?

So many times when we present on behavioral styles, we are asked, "Is my behavior in-born... genetic or does it come from the environment that I was brought up in?" Talk about controversy! There are so many arguments for both schools of thought, so we simply say, "There are arguments for both. What we know is that your behavioral style is affecting your referability in your business right now."

In most cases, our audience members, whether at a large keynote presentation or a 100-person Room Full of Referrals® session, can identify with the fact that it's more important to learn how to manage their behavioral styles, instead of trying to figure out how they came to have that style.

The other big question we often get is why do we call these traits behavioral styles instead of personality styles? We love this one because it's much easier to define. *Personality* is more closely related to psychology than behavior. But you don't have to become a psychologist to observe people's behavior, which is simply how they act and react in different situations.

If someone is impatient, they tend to be impatient in most circumstances. If they are encouraging, they can be encouraging no matter where they are. If they need a lot of details to make a decision, that will always be part of their decision-making process. You get the picture, right?

The first step in understanding behavioral styles is to understand you. So we are going to have you start by taking a very simple assessment. This will give you an idea which of the four behavioral styles you are. As we shared earlier, everyone is a blend of all four styles, in varying degrees of intensity. Keep that mind as we have you declare a dominant style – you're a blend, too! As you read the rest of this book we will focus on your most dominant style.

Here is where Tony's expertise comes into play. Tony is known for being the creator of the Platinum Rule®[3]. Most of us understand the Golden Rule: "Do unto others as you as you would have others do unto you." However, the Platinum Rule® is:

"Do unto others as they would have you do unto them."

Here's an even simpler way to phrase it: "Treat others the way that they want to be treated." Basically, we should never assume that people are just like us and want to be treated in the same way.

Praise for the Platinum Rule®

"Dr. Tony Alessandra's work brilliantly provides effective insights for improving communication in any and all situations."
John Gray, Ph.D., *Author, Men Are From Mars, Women Are From Venus*

"[This concept] is Chicken Soup for the Head! It gives fun and useful insights as to how to enhance both business and personal relationships. Tony Alessandra is a master at this and I recommend that you (listen to) it often."
Jack Canfield, *Co-author, Chicken Soup for the Soul*

"[This concept] breaks all the old rules of communications. It is full of take action strategies that cut like a laser to the heart of the human personality... yours and your customer's. Don't underestimate (its) power. A learning and earning tool for the times."
Harvey Mackay, *Author, Swim with the Sharks Without Being Eaten Alive*

"[This] is the priceless key to unlocking the door to empowerment, productivity and all business and personal relationships. It is simply the most important leadership concept I have learned in all of my life!"
Denis Waitley, *Author, Empires of the Mind and The Psychology of Winning*

[3] The Platinum Rule® is a registered trademark of Dr. Tony Alessandra. Used here with permission.

When Tony was a young man, he learned this lesson first-hand when he moved from New York to San Diego. He practiced the Golden Rule verbatim by treating the people in San Diego the way he liked to be treated… as a New Yorker.

He came on too strong; he was too assertive and just "too fast" for most of the laid-back people on the West Coast. He rubbed many people the wrong way, which prompted them to "dig in their heels" and few responded positively to his requests.

Fortunately, he soon realized that people are diverse and each needs to be treated differently. As he became more self-aware, he coined the phrase, "The Platinum Rule®."

The Platinum Rule is a more sensitive version of the more ancient axiom, the Golden Rule. That is, learn to understand the behaviors of others and interact with them in a style that is best for them, not just for you.

"Just three days after participating in a Room Full of Referrals program, I used the information I learned! My husband and I did a presentation to 40 real estate agents.

"Afterwards an agent, who I recognized to be a Go-Getter/Examiner, came up to me. Without asking anything remotely nice or friendly (in my mind), she began interrogating me, asking if we were insured, bonded, specifics on pricing and on and on. I met her on her level. Answered every question she fired at me and did away with the small talk or chit chat I may have engaged in before learning about behavioral styles.

"Instead of feeling intimidated or un-liked, I realized she just needed the facts and to be able to check off my answers on her invisible check list because of her behavioral style. I left the conversation knowing I treated her the way that SHE wanted to be treated!"

Elisa Chieffo • California Steam Clean • www.calsteamclean.com

You need to adapt so that, while retaining your own identity, you can lead others in the way they like to follow, speak to them the way they are comfortable listening and sell to them the way they prefer to buy.

When you understand your own style and how it differs from the styles of others, you can adapt your approach to stay "on the same wavelength" with them. Your ideas do not have to change, but you can change the way you present your ideas. We call this adaptability.

Adaptable people realize there is a difference between their inner self (who they are) and their external behavior (how they choose to act). Adaptability is simply changing your behavior, not your personality, values or beliefs.

Adaptable people consciously decide to modify their behaviors to a particular person, a situation or an event. Less adaptable people, on the other hand, respond in a more habitual manner, regardless of whether the response is likely to be appropriate or effective or not.

Tony Notes a Critical Distinction

The Platinum Rule® is based upon observable behaviors, NOT "personalities" or "temperaments." This distinction is critical because human beings may change their behavior in the middle of a conversation.

When you learn to adapt to the behavior that you are witnessing, you will stay in rapport with that person. People's personalities are deeply ingrained and slow to change, but behaviors can change in the blink of an eye. The way a person is acting at each moment in time will dictate how you should be interacting with them.

The goal of the Platinum Rule® is personal chemistry and productive relationships. You do not have to change your personality. You do not have to roll over and submit to others. You simply have to understand what drives people and recognize your options for dealing with them.

A Story from Dawn: Selling to Someone's Style

Recently I needed four "sandwich board" signs for my businesses. A local BNI member in the industry was referred to me. He came over to my home and unloaded seven or eight different signs from his truck. I listened to him talk about two of the signs for a couple of minutes before I stopped him.

"Matt, have you ever heard about behavioral styles?" I asked.

"Well, I have heard a lot of the other BNI chapter members talk about it," he replied. "But I have not taken your Room Full of Referrals® program yet."

"Can I give you a bit of advice about my style?"

"Sure," he said cautiously.

I continued: "I am someone who really doesn't want any details. I need to know which sign is the best and how much it costs, whether I have to put it together or you'll do it for me and how fast can I get them. Tell me all that, and I will make a decision now. You'll leave with a check in your hands for four signs."

I let him digest that for a bit, and then said, "So, here's what I'd like to do. You select your top two signs. I am going to go back inside and make a phone call. When I come back you can tell me the differences between the two, the prices and how quickly I can get them. Then we'll be done here. Does that sound okay?"

He was a little taken back that I was so direct but replied that it would be fine. I went inside to make my call, and when I came back out Matt said, "This one has these features, this one does not. This one costs X amount and this one is $20 more because I have to put it together. This one I can get you in four days, and this one takes seven. My recommendation is that you get this one."

"Sounds great," I said. "How much for four of them with these logos on it? And can I write you a check?"

Done. Sold. Easy.

You see, if I hadn't shared with Matt how to sell to me, I could have felt that he wasted my time and not had an overall great experience with him. The next time I needed a sign, I would have been less likely to contact him due to how I felt about the first appointment.

Every time we begin a conversation, an appointment or any engagement with others, we always bring our own behavioral style to the table. It's how we're wired. Matt did nothing wrong and, in fact, is a great guy. He simply began selling to me in a way that he enjoys versus what I prefer. Today, I would always go back and buy from Matt as now he understands how to work with me and treat me the way that I want to be treated!

What Style Are You?

Let's find out what style you are. Keep in mind that this is a very basic assessment. (If you are interested in going beyond the basics, we will provide you with a chance to receive a more thorough assessment that includes a 27-page report all about you. We will share with you how you can get a special discount on that report later in this chapter.)

Once you identify your most dominant behavioral style, we are also going to have you assess where you are in your referral marketing efforts as it applies to behavioral styles on the next page.

Your Behavioral Style Assessment

Instructions: Below you have two columns, with opposite behaviors. Please put a check mark in the box by the statement that best describes you for each pair. When you're finished you'll add up your check marks for each section of questions.

I tend to act in the following ways:

- ☐ Usually react slowly/deliberately
- ☐ Usually ask questions or speaks more tentatively and indirectly
- ☐ Usually contribute infrequently to group conversations
- ☐ Likes to think over decision before making them
- ☐ More patient than average
- ☐ Come across as more reserved
- ☐ Risk-avoider
- ☐ Tend to listen more than talk
- ☐ Usually respond to conflict slowly and indirectly

- ☐ Usually react quickly/decisively
- ☐ Usually make emphatic statements or directly expresses opinions
- ☐ Usually contribute frequently to group conversations
- ☐ Make quick decisions
- ☐ Less patient than average
- ☐ Come across as more assertive
- ☐ Risk-taker
- ☐ Tend to talk more than listen
- ☐ Usually respond to conflict quickly and directly

Please add up your total check marks for each column.

______***total*** ______***total***

The left column is slower-paced, and the right column is more fast-paced.

Based on my totals, I am more:

slower-paced or fast-paced
(circle one)

I tend to act in the following ways:

- ☐ Find it easy to share/discuss personal feelings with others
- ☐ Tend to take the initiative and introduce self to others
- ☐ Usually responsive to others' agendas, interests and concerns
- ☐ Usually interact with others in a relaxed and informal manner
- ☐ Usually prefer to work with others as part of a group or team
- ☐ Tend to focus primarily on relationships over tasks
- ☐ When making decisions, rely more on feelings over facts
- ☐ Easy to get to know
- ☐ Open to establishing relationships with people

- ☐ Keep personal feelings private, sharing only when necessary
- ☐ Tend to wait for others to introduce themselves to him/her
- ☐ Usually directed toward your own agenda, interests and concerns
- ☐ Usually interact with others in a more formal and proper manner
- ☐ Prefer to work independently
- ☐ Tend to focus primarily on tasks over relationships
- ☐ When making decisions, rely more on facts over feelings
- ☐ Take time to get to know him/her
- ☐ Guarded about establishing relationships with people

Please add up your total check marks for each column.

______***total*** ______***total***

The left column is people-oriented, and the right column is more task-oriented.

Based on my totals, I am more:

people-oriented or task-oriented
(circle one)

So, what does all of this translate to? Please select from the following to figure out your most dominant behavioral style.

If you chose that you are slower-paced and people-oriented, your style is **NURTURER**

> Nurturers tend to be caring, thoughtful people who enjoy helping others and strongly dislike confrontation as they do not like to hurt people's feelings.

If you chose that you are fast-paced and people-oriented, your style is **PROMOTER**

> Promoters tend to be gregarious, fun people who enjoy excitement and the spotlight and are very concerned with people liking them.

If you chose that you are slower-paced and task-oriented, your style is **EXAMINER**

> Examiners tend to be very methodical, process-oriented people who enjoy completing tasks and dislike anything with too much hype that is not based on facts.

If you chose that you are fast-paced and task-oriented, your style is **GO-GETTER**

> Go-Getters tend to be very driven, challenge-oriented people who enjoy winning at everything and strongly dislike being wrong about anything.

This simple assessment is important because it will help you begin to understand who you are and ensure you get the most that you can from this book. Again, although you've determined your most dominant style, this does not mean that you do not have any of the other qualities within you.

Determining the Behavioral Styles of Others

Just understanding the four qualifiers above, fast-paced, slower-paced, task-oriented and people-oriented, can definitely help you to identify other people's style. Think about your friends or associates; are they fast-paced or slower-paced?

Do they talk fast, walk fast and make quick decisions? Or, do they take their time, speak a bit slower and think about things longer? Are they more people-driven or task-driven? Meaning, are they always focused on accomplishing something, writing a list and checking it off and working on projects? Or, are they more concerned with talking about the people involved, not what the project is?

Based on these questions, are you able to make some guesses about people in your life and what style they might be?

A Story from Tony: Two People in Line

I love to watch people, especially in public places. It's where I get some of my great stories. I was watching a situation in a bank the other day. Everybody is in this long line – there must have been 20 people. They have one teller open. And yet there are two other tellers. I don't know what they're doing. But they're sitting there.

So I watch a direct person and an indirect person come to the end of line. Nobody likes lines. But they handle it very differently. *(Note from Dawn: Direct is referred to as fast-paced elsewhere in the book. Indirect is slower-paced.)*

The indirect person walked in head down, slow and reserved. He looked up, sighed at the long line, and muttered to himself about the two tellers just sitting there when there are 20 people in line. "I'm going to be late for work," he said to himself, shaking his head.

Of course, a direct person handled it very differently. You can spot a direct person, by the way, just from their pace. He walked in fast and when he saw the line, he immediately complained to everyone within ear shot. "I can't believe it," he said, look at the line. And, "I'm going to be late for work."

When he found out about the two tellers just sitting there – he – in a loud voice - immediately asked them to open up. And you know what, they did.

Of course, we're going to go into depth on each of the behavioral styles in the next chapter, so you will gain a lot more information about your most dominant style. What we really want you to learn here is that when you begin to identify someone else's style it really helps when you start with fast-paced, slower-paced, task-oriented and people-oriented. In fact, let's do that now.

Write down the names of three people who are:

Fast-Paced

1.

2.

3.

Slower-Paced

1.

2.

3.

Now, take the same people and ask yourself if they are people-oriented or task-oriented. List their name below appropriately.

People-Oriented

1.

2.

3.

Task-Oriented

1.

2.

3.

Now, you can go back and look at the titles for each group above and each person's most dominant style. Pretty simple, right?

Here is a quick question: From reading just the couple of stories that Dawn has shared, can you identify her style? Remember to think fast-paced versus slower-paced and people-oriented versus task-oriented. What is your guess? Circle one:

Nurturer **Promoter** **Examiner** **Go-Getter**

No, we are not going to give you the answer just yet. We just want you to be aware that with just the information you have received so far, you can begin to assess the behavioral styles of other people! Later in the book, we will also have you guess Tony's and Ivan's styles.

Now, because this was such a simple assessment, we would like to share with you a way to truly gain a better understanding! If you would like to take an assessment that will give you a 27-page report all about you, we encourage you to do that now. Please do not read any further if you are going to purchase the assessment. Order it now and take it before reading the rest of the book.

"We just secured an account with a Canada-based corporation that operates over 3,000 spas and salons in the U.S. and Canada.

"Honestly, without the exposure to behavioral styles and the Room Full of Referrals™ program, I would not have made it through this process with them. We just completed a test with the first of their five spas, and have been handed phase II which has 83 more.

"The past month I have dealt with more behavioral styles than I ever have in my life! Adapting and working with them all has been eye-opening. Thanks for helping me land this incredibly huge account for my company."

Kelly Richardson • President, Be Bronze LLC • www.bebronze.com

(If you'd like to keep reading, turn to the section "Behavioral Styles and Referral Marketing" on page 35.)

Here are some of the benefits of owning your report:

- You will have a more detailed understanding of your most dominant style.
- You will get a clearer picture of how the blends work together.
- You will gain ideas around adapting to others.
- You will learn techniques to making your conversations easier.
- You will begin to be able to identify other styles in your life.
- You will have a better understanding of the appropriate actions to take with others.
- You will absolutely see how you can save time in building stronger relationships.
- You will become more efficient at selecting the "right" relationships for you.
- You will be able to help others feel more comfortable in networking situations.
- Lastly, you will acquire one of the most important skills ever... understanding other people and why they do what they do!

To complete your online assessment and instantly receive your 27-page report all about you, please go to www.RoomFullofReferrals.com. The assessment is valued at $69.95. Simply click on the "Take Assessment Here" button and you will receive a credit of $21.95 – the price you paid for this book! Subtract your credit of $21.95 and for just $48.00 you will receive the most valuable information ever... who you truly are and how you can adapt to others! Remember, your product is people!

For those of you more immersed in referral activities, you may also contact the Referral Institute headquarters to receive a 90-minute consultation on your assessment and how it is affecting your referability. Our consultants can offer a 360-degree view of up to 100 contacts and how they view your behavioral style. The 100 contacts are graphed into your assessment and our consultants can show you how and why your relationships are exactly where they are in your referral marketing efforts. Plus, they can give you tips and techniques about how to take specific referral relationships to the next level.

To contact the Referral Institute, please send an email to: office@referralinstitute.com with "Platinum Rule® Consultation Requested" in the subject line. One of our representatives will contact you about next steps. Consultations average $249 and save our clients hours and hours of frustration of wondering why their relationships aren't gaining them the referrals they are looking for!

When you take the online assessment be sure to spend some time reading through the report before reading this book further. It will help you dramatically as we cover more information throughout this book. It's very eye-opening to understanding how your style is affecting everything you do. It will help you in so many ways.

Keep it handy, don't just put it aside in a bookcase somewhere. If you're going on a big appointment, for instance, you may want to look over the adapting section in the report you now have to see how you can adapt your style to the person you are meeting.

"I'm quite passionate about what I do and, prior to taking the Room Full of Referrals™ program, I would always take the time to educate my patients in great detail. What I didn't realize is that I was catering to my behavioral style and not always to the patient, who often does not need or want that much information.

"The training I have received at the Referral Institute, and particularly the Room Full of Referrals™ program, have created a pivotal shift in my ability to better communicate with my patients in THEIR language, and to better understand their needs. I highly recommend it!"

Dr. Steven A. Battaglino, Owner • Battaglino Family Chiropractic
www.battaglinochiropractic.com

And now, back to our regularly-scheduled reading...

Behavioral Styles and Referral Marketing

Now that you have identified your most dominant behavioral style, let's get an idea of how proficient you are with applying this information to referral marketing. We have mentioned referral marketing several times, and we would like to take just a moment to define what we truly mean by *your referral marketing efforts*. We are not speaking about network marketing, multi-level marketing or direct sales. We are focusing this book on how you are currently generating referrals for your business.

As business owners or entrepreneurs, we should all have written business plans for our companies, right? Well, we certainly hope that you have one. If not, look for a referral to a great business coach and have them help you create a business plan.

Now, within your business plan you will have sections dealing with revenue, expenses, forecasts, ideal clients and, of course, a marketing plan. There are several ways people can market their businesses: PR, cold calls, advertising, word of mouth, etc. Each type of marketing should have a mini plan behind it. How much time, effort and money does each one need?

So our question is: Do you have a written referral marketing plan for your business? No? Well, join the club. We estimate that 99.5% of the business owners we talk to do not have a written referral marketing plan for their company. The 0.5% who do have a written referral marketing plan tend to be our Referral Institute clients!

What we would like for you to do next is take another simple assessment based on your knowledge of behavioral styles and referral marketing techniques. You will take this assessment again at the end of the book to see how much you have learned! Please answer the following questions based on your current level of knowledge. Please circle the number that best fits you!

- I understand the strengths and weaknesses of all four behavioral styles.

Lowest 0 1 2 3 4 5 *Highest*

- I understand how my own style is affecting my referability.

Lowest 0 1 2 3 4 5 *Highest*

- I can identify the styles of my top 10 referral sources.

Lowest 0 1 2 3 4 5 *Highest*

- When at networking functions, I can observe the four different styles.

Lowest 0 1 2 3 4 5 *Highest*

- When I meet someone, I can identify his or her top two styles within 20-30 seconds.

Lowest 0 1 2 3 4 5 *Highest*

- I understand the language of all four styles.

Lowest 0 1 2 3 4 5 *Highest*

- When I meet someone, I can immediately begin to speak to them in their language.

Lowest 0 1 2 3 4 5 *Highest*

- When I meet someone, I am able to change my pace, hand gestures and tonality.

Lowest 0 1 2 3 4 5 *Highest*

- When I meet someone, I am able to manage the conversation so that they appreciate the conversation.

Lowest 0 1 2 3 4 5 *Highest*

- When working with referral sources, I always adapt to their style.

Lowest 0 1 2 3 4 5 *Highest*

- When working with referral sources, I am aware of how they want to be trained by style.

Lowest 0 1 2 3 4 5 *Highest*

Continue on next page

- When working with referral sources, I follow up with them based on their behavioral style.

Lowest 0 1 2 3 4 5 *Highest*

- When working with referral sources, I am able to have them teach me what style their referred prospect is before I meet with them.

Lowest 0 1 2 3 4 5 *Highest*

- When working with referral sources, I always reward them based on their behavioral style.

Lowest 0 1 2 3 4 5 *Highest*

- When working with referral sources, I am always aware of their style and how to serve them as we work together.

Lowest 0 1 2 3 4 5 *Highest*

Next, please add up your points: ______
Then look below to see your current level of knowledge of behavioral styles and how they relate to referral marketing.

Inspired to Learn (1 - 20 points)

You could be hearing about behavioral styles for the very first time, and, if so, we congratulate you for being open to learning new information! Maybe you have heard a bit about it, but have never taken any kind of formal assessment to see and understand what style you are.

Nonetheless, you have gone this far, and this is the only book that we know of to relate behavioral styles to referral marketing. Keep reading… you will be amazed at what you will learn about yourself and about others! You are in the unconscious incompetence stage – you don't know what you don't know AND are willing to learn!

Ready to Learn More (21 - 45 points)

Our guess is that you have probably taken some sort of assessment in your life, and you are aware that behavioral styles exist. You may even realize when you really click with some people and clash with others. You are probably fairly focused on networking and referrals. You are wondering more about the "how-tos" of implementing this information so you know what your next step is. In many cases, you may figure out after the fact that the reason you didn't get the deal or have a good conversation was because of a lack of understanding of a person's behavioral style. You are in the conscious incompetence stage and on your way to improving!

Ready to Implement it More Often (46 - 65 points)

You stand firm in understanding who you are, and you can identify other people's styles as well. You are mostly aware of behavioral styles and can adapt the style of others to an adequate level. You are very active in networking and developing your referral sources. You have a huge desire to do 100% of your business by referral. You are at a conscious competence stage but looking to continually get better and better so you don't have to think about it.

You are a K.I.D. (66 - 75 points)

You have the Knowledge, you are Implementing it, and you are Developing long-term referral relationships with it! You have spent years learning this information, and lots of time and energy has been focused on applying it when working with your referral sources. You are someone who is constantly aware, constantly identifying and constantly adapting your own style to serve others. Congratulations for honoring others! You are probably producing over 60% of your business by referral. You are working in the unconscious competence stage and the percentage of your business by referral only gets higher and higher from here.

The Four Stages of Competence

If you have never learned the four stages of learning before, here is a short overview of the journey from unconscious incompetence to unconscious competence.

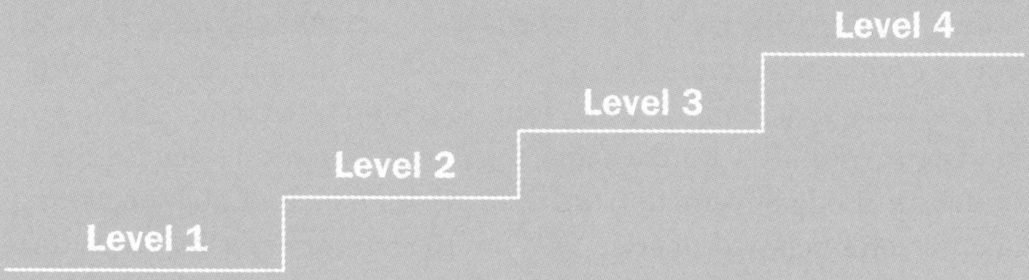

Level 1 – Unconscious Incompetence

You have no knowledge or skills in the subject. And you are completely unaware of that fact.

Level 2 – Conscious Incompetence

You realize there are many skills you need and much knowledge to learn. You might struggle with this as you now understand how little you know.

Level 3 – Conscious Competence

Armed with appropriate knowledge and skills, you are able complete tasks competently and are getting better and better. Your confidence is rising.

Level 4 – Unconscious Competence

You no longer have to concentrate to perform activities successfully. You complete jobs with excellent results as a matter of habit. You are extremely confident in your abilities.

Tony Provides a Real-World Example

Can you remember when you first learned how to drive a car? Before you learned how, you were in the "ignorance" stage, or unconscious incompetence. You did not know how to drive the car, and you didn't even know why you didn't know how to drive it. When you first went out with an instructor to learn how to drive you arrived at the second phase: awareness, or conscious incompetence.

You still couldn't drive, but because of your new awareness of the automobile and its parts, you were consciously aware of why you couldn't. At this point, the "awareness" stage, you at least realized what you had to do to acquire the competency to drive.

With some additional practice and guidance, you were able to become competent in driving the car through recognition of what you had to do. However, you had to be consciously aware of what you were doing with all of the mechanical aspects of the car as well as with your body.

You had to be consciously aware of turning on your blinker signals well before you executed a turn. You had to remember to monitor the traffic behind you in your rearview mirror. You kept both hands on the wheel and noted your car's position relative to the center line road divider. You were consciously aware of all of these things as you competently drove. This third phase, conscious competence, is the hardest stage - the one in which your people may want to give up.

Now, think of the last time that you drove. Were you consciously aware of all of the actions mentioned above? Of course not! Most of us, after driving awhile, progress to a level of unconscious competence. This is the level where we can do something well and don't have to think about the steps. They come "naturally" because they've been so well practiced that they've shifted to automatic pilot.

Now that you have taken both the behavioral style assessment and the referral marketing assessment, let's define more of the qualities and traits of each of the four behavioral styles. This will help you in understanding how your behavioral style is affecting your referability.

CHAPTER 4
Understanding the Four Major Behavioral Styles

After realizing how powerful the concept of behavioral styles is to referral marketing, their core business, the partners of the Referral Institute decided to develop an in-house system for their members. As we mentioned earlier in the book, there are many different ways to "title" the four major styles.

Dawn spearheaded this effort to create their own titles that would speak to their audience and have credibility in the business world. In crafting the four different behavioral styles, we have strived to do several things:

- Inspire positivity
- Ensure clarity between the four styles
- Make the styles instantly understandable to anyone
- Create a picture of the person described
- Have the titles be congruent with people's actions while networking, which is, of course, our niche

Once we selected the titles, our next step was to get validation from an expert. Of course, we went to Tony as we knew we would want to utilize his assessment tools. All of the Referral Institute Partners were in Big Bear, California at a Partner's retreat and Tony also came up to work with us. As soon as we shared the titles we'd been working on with him he said, "They're perfect! Clear, focused, completely on-track with what you do and simple."

Here are the four main behavioral styles, complete with a short definition and description.

Go-Getter

Definition: A hustling, enterprising type of person. The Go-Getter would be the equivalent of the D in DiSC®.

Go-Getters tend to be very results-oriented, driven, fast-paced and impatient. They have a "get it done now" attitude. They attend networking events to gain new business and look to meet the most successful people at the event.

As Tony says, Go-Getters "believe in expedience and are not afraid to bend the rules. They figure it is easier to beg forgiveness than to ask permission. They are so focused that they can appear aloof. They are so driven that they forget to take the time to smell the roses."

Promoter

Definition: An active supporter, someone who urges the adoption of, or attempts to sell or popularize someone or something. The Promoter would be the equivalent of the i in DiSC® language.

Promoters tend to be very positive, friendly and "happy go lucky" type of people. They love to be on the go and are okay with having lots of irons in the fire. They avoid confrontations and seek fun in everything they do! They attend networking events to hang out, meet new people, talk to their friends and make sure they are "seen" at the event.

"[Promoters] would rather "schmooze" with clients over lunch than work on a proposal in the office," says Tony. "They are idea-people and dreamers who excel at getting others excited about their vision. They are risk-takers who are not inclined to do their homework or check out information and base many of their decisions on intuition."

Nurturer

Definition: Someone who gives tender care and protection to a person or thing, especially to help it grow or develop. The Nurturer would be the equivalent to the S in DiSC® language.

Nurturers tend to be very patient, kind, caring and helpful people. They are great listeners and tend to enjoy things at a slower pace than the Go-Getters and Promoters. They do not liked to be pushed or rushed into things and appreciate quality time with people. They attend networking functions to connect with people they already know, meet a few down to earth people and focus on deepening their relationships.

As Tony says, "[Nurturers'] relaxed dispositions make them approachable and warm. They develop strong networks of people who are willing to be mutually supportive and reliable. They are excellent team players. But they are risk-averse and may tolerate an unpleasant environment rather than risk a change."

Examiner

Definition: A person who inspects or analyzes a person, place or thing in detail, while testing their knowledge or skill by asking questions. The Examiner would be the equivalent of the C in the DiSC® language.

Examiners tend to be very thorough, efficient, task-driven people. They seek information and knowledge and love to check things off their "to do" list. Because Examiners need a lot of information, they tend to make decisions more slowly than the Go-Getters and Promoters. They have a propensity towards perfectionism. Examiners tend to be very good conversationalists as they know a lot about a lot of topics. They attend networking functions only to market their business and, once they achieve their goal for the evening, they usually leave the event as quickly as possible.

Says Tony, "[Examiners] are always in control of their emotions (note the poker-faces of many *Jeopardy!* contestants) and may become uncomfortable around people who are less self-contained; i.e., emotional and bubbly like [Promoters]. They tend to see the serious, complex side of situations. Their intelligence and natural wit, however, gives them unique, quick and off-the-wall senses of humor."

Can You Guess the Styles?

Next, we would like to see if you can guess the styles of the four people in the following stories from Dawn. Yes, we understand that you have just a tiny bit of information about the four different styles. But we are confident that with what you know so far and the description in each of the stories below, you will be able to identify the person's dominant behavioral style.

Make sure to read the stories in their entirety as it provides a deep picture into each person's style. Quick note: Some of you will find yourselves unusually annoyed with a story, believing the length is obscenely long and wondering why we needed to give you so much detail. We get it, and that is your style showing through! Others may read one of the stories and think "that is just arrogant and rude" and that is *your* style showing through. Take note of how you feel reading each of the stories. It will identify something about your own style!

Dawn's First Story: The Box of Tissues

There are 32 people in attendance at our Target Market class. I am about to discuss something we call the Emotionally Charged Connection™. It's the reason people are passionate about their businesses, and it connects their clients and referral sources to them in a way that inspires loyalty and an eagerness to follow that person anywhere!

When individuals discover their Emotionally Charged Connection™, it really is a deep, emotional experience. When people share their Emotionally Charged Connections, that same emotion can come up again. And, even for the most accomplished presenters, they may get choked up a bit or a tear may be shed.

Now, back to the story. I'm leading the Target Market class, talking about my Emotionally Charged Connection™, when it happens. My eyes are welling up, I have a lump in my throat, and, yep, a tear drop rolls down my cheek. As I take a long deep breath this wonderful man from the back of the room brings me up some tissue. I finish telling my story, fighting the tears. The class ends, and he comes up to me.

"Thaaannnkkk Yoouuu," he says as he grabs my hands and clasps them together with his. "I cannot share with you enough how revealing today's class was for me. To see you be that vulnerable in front of all of us was something I am sure you didn't enjoy necessarily, but I truly feel I know you much better as a person now, more than I have from seeing you at different events in the past two years"

"Awww," I say, holding back the tears again as I clench my jaw. "It was very nice of you to get me that tissue. I think next time I should just have a box sitting up here."

"You just let me know when you do this again, and I will bring them to you!" he exclaims.

Double awww, I think to myself! And then say, "You are tooooo kind. Thank you for not making me feel awkward about this. It's not the most comfortable thing to do."

"On the contrary," he says, "I thought it was your best moment. I am so much more inspired to help you now that I know why you are so passionate about it. Thank you for sharing."

By this time I am ready to be done with the conversation. I've had enough of the touchy-feely scenario. (Hey, don't judge me, remember it's how I am wired.) Before I can politely excuse myself from the conversation, he says, "Well, I am sorry I took up so much of your time," as if the 90 seconds that had transpired was a lot of time, "I am sure you have other, more important people to talk to."

I touch him on the shoulder and ask, "Wait one second; the most important thing to me is that YOU received valuable information tonight for YOUR business... did you?"

"Oh yes, of course I did."

"Then can I ask you a favor?"

"Sure," he replies.

"If you truly want to help me, then help your business and USE this information to make positive, long-term shifts to get your business to the next level. If you do that then I can share your story of success. There is nothing else that excites me more than sharing success stories. I would love to do that for you!"

He smiles brightly, nods his head and says "thank you" one more time before walking toward the door.

What style was he? ______________________

Dawn's Second Story: High Energy

I'm in a room of 340 people and during a break I walk around to say hi to the attendees. One happy and energetic gal, very pretty with bright pink lips, walks right up to me and says, "Oh, I just have to introduce myself, I am ______. My friend ______ said you were wonderful, and she was soooooo right! She was the one who got me started in BNI and is one of my mentors. She is just fantastic, she loves you and, after seeing you present, I love you, too! You were fabulous!"

"Wow," I say, noticing that she is still shaking my hand. "That is so incredibly nice of you to say. What was it that you liked the most?"

"Your energy and passion is contagious. It is so important to me that I work with people like that; it just makes things so much easier."

Adjusting my style, I say, "Oh, totally! Isn't it a drag to refer people that don't really care about their business or have absolutely no passion?"

"Yep, and I simply don't do it. I won't," she says. "It's no fun at all for me or my clients."

I can't continue this conversation for much longer – I need to keep moving - so I say, "Listen, I just want to let you know I have noticed your smile from the front of the room. Are you gonna keep that up for me for the rest of the day because it really feeds me!?"

"Of course I will," she says with an incredibly big smile on her face!

As I turn to walk away, I hear her say to someone at her table, "WOW, she noticed my smile. She is so cool!"

What style was she? ______________________

Dawn's Third Story: Time or Money

As I am getting ready for a BNI Visitor Day, I see him. He is the second person to arrive and is 20 minutes early. He has his newspaper under his arm. And he's wearing a sports coat; you know, the tan fuzzy ones, and it looks 25 years old. He is standing just inside the room past the registration table surveying the room. He has his own cup of coffee, and you can just tell he's deliberating where he should sit. He selects a seat in the back left corner and begins to read his newspaper. There is a bustling energy in the room as people come in that simply does not affect or include him. He is extremely focused on his newspaper.

Now, I see several BNI members try to talk to him but notice none of them spend more than a minute, and they all stayed standing. As I get ready for the program, I see him fold up his newspaper at 6:58. See, he was told the program would start at 7 a.m. He looks toward the front of the room, and I smile slightly and nod. He barely nods back but does acknowledge me. I set my papers down and meander through the crowd towards him.

I pull up a chair two seats away and say, "Hello, I'm Dawn." As I stretch out my hand, he says, "Hello, I'm Jerry."

I ask him if anyone shared how the visitor day was structured. He says no very quickly with a hint of discontent in his voice. I thought that might be the case, so I offer to give him all the details. He agrees with a simple yes. Oh boy Dawn, I think to myself, you had better change this person around or there is no way he will enjoy the program today.

"The first part of the meeting, the open networking section, does start at 7 a.m.," I explain. "This is where people can interact to understand a bit more about their businesses and see how they might be able to generate referrals for each other more efficiently. To be most effective during this part of the program, I suggest you speak with someone who is in a similar field as yours. What is it that you do for a living?"

"I am a CPA," he replies.

Oh, of course you are, I think to myself. After some prompting, he reveals he's been practicing for 27 years, which I mention our financial advisor Cheryl will be very impressed with. But he's still giving me just three- to four-word answers. I take a deep breath. I continue telling him about the event.

"Next, the president will call the meeting to order at 7:15 on the nose. Our agenda is timed to the minute. You'll hear some general reports. There is an educational part to the agenda with tips and techniques on how to network with ease. All members give a detailed description of the specific type of referral they are looking for this week. And this morning, we have a 20-minute speaker who is well-known in the area for her success and is in the top 14% of directors in the organization.

"Then we come to our most important part of the meeting where we pass legitimate referrals to one another. After, we have a few more reports, and then the president will excuse all visitors so they can identify if BNI is a good fit for them or not. Does that help you understand what will happen this morning?"

"Yes, that is completely clear. I wish someone would have explained that to me earlier!" he says with the discontent coming back in his voice.

Wanting to get him off of the topic, I note that he seems to be done with his newspaper and ask if it would be appropriate for me to introduce him to Cheryl. I explain she'll be able to help him understand what she might be looking for in a CPA to refer business to.

"Clearly that would be a good use of my time. Yes, please introduce me," he states emphatically.

I go on my way make the introduction, and with our CPA now comfortable, all is fine and dandy. I make sure to ask Cheryl to sit next to him in case he has any questions during the meeting.

Mark, the chapter president, comes up to me and says, "Wow, how did you get that guy to move? He was super grumpy with me and said all he wanted to do was read his newspaper."

"Oh, I just worked within his behavioral style, and he was putty in my hands" I say. "See, we interrupted his normal schedule by having an event so early. His first and only task when arriving here was to read his paper. Once he accomplished that, I showed him the layout of the morning and suggested a way that he could use his time very effectively... that's all."

"How did you know to do all of that?" asks Mark.

"I have spent 20 years learning about behavioral styles and how to honor others," I explain.

"Well," he says, "it worked. Look at him and Cheryl, it looks like they are having a great conversation. Yep, I think he is pretty happy now that he can talk to someone in a similar industry."

After the event, Jerry is speaking with Cheryl, and as I walk by, he stops me.

"Dawn, I wanted to get a moment with you before you leave, is that OK?" he asks. "I was really impressed with your presentation today and enjoyed understanding how to apply for membership. But I was most impressed with the fact that you didn't boast about yourself when we first met this morning. Instead, you let me come to my own conclusion. After hearing your biography, I am very impressed with your success and wanted to let you know that I can see the effectiveness, but I really need some time to think to see if I can make all of the commitments before joining this group."

"Jerry, first of all, you don't need to prove anything to me," I assure him. "We know we have a very effective way of helping business owners generate more referrals. It looks like you and Cheryl hit if off nicely. So, if nothing else, that is probably a good connection for you, right?"

"Yes, of course it is."

"So, if nothing else happens from today, was it worth your time being here this morning?"

"Yes, I learned a lot that I can use in my business."

"Well, then you have time to think about your commitments. But remember, your competition is eligible to apply for membership at any time. I would be remiss if I didn't remind you."

Then, after a long pause, I ask Jerry exactly what he wants to think about, the money or the time?

"Oh, it's not the money," he says. "I have been doing this for 27 years and have a very profitable practice. But when I make a commitment to a project, I want it to be perfect. I need to check my schedule, see if I am going to miss any meetings and make sure I can adhere to the BNI policies and procedures

"So, you probably need a couple of weeks to figure this out right?"

"Oh, definitely not, I will make time in my schedule today to look at a ROI plan, speak with my wife tonight, and make sure that I can go to that orientation program within the next 60 days. I will be able to let Cheryl know my decision by Thursday at 9 a.m."

"Ah, okay, well it sounds like you have it all under control," I say as I mosey off, knowing I asked lots of great questions to get him to take the next steps.

Hurray! I hear from Cheryl at about 9:30 on Thursday that Jerry had just left her office after having dropped off an application for membership into BNI! Double Hurray!

What style was he? ___________________________

Dawn's Fourth Story: Flash in the Pan?

Several years ago I was speaking to a group of five people at the end of a BNI chapter meeting. They were all guests looking at the possibility of applying for membership to the chapter.

One gentleman, let's call him Ray, was dressed in a navy suit with a bright red tie, lace-up shiny black shoes that looked brand new, and short dark hair - every single strand was in place. He wore a shiny gold watch and a gold wedding band with a single 1-carat diamond.

Ray raised his hand and asked for an application. I give him one but mentioned we would be covering a few other things first. He begins to fill out the form, and I keep talking to the whole group. I ask everyone what their ability is to bring in qualified referrals, and Ray immediately answers that he'll probably be the number one person in the chapter. Oh, okay, I think to myself, Mr. Showoff. He continues to brag about his large network and how much people listen to him and take his advice.

Alrighty, then, I think to myself. I collect the rest of the answers, which are nowhere near as arrogant as Ray's answer comes across. He finishes his application, looks at his watch, and says, "Do you mind if I just turn this in? I have an appointment I must get to."

Meanwhile three others are filling out their application and are nowhere close to being finished. I accept Ray's application, and after asking him if he has any further questions, he comes back with, "No, I get it. I got it from the first 10 minutes. I think it's a great organization, I live on referrals, I can give lots of referrals, and from everything I know this group is the largest and the best in the area. That's who I want to be networking with.

"If I'm correct about all of that," he says, "then I will simply pay for my application and look forward to being inducted as soon as possible."

You're correct," I say. "They are the largest, strongest chapter in the area, and they are very serious about accepting professionals who will be productive members. Here is the credit card slip. Fill that out and you are free to go."

"Perfect, thanks for your time, Dawn."

"No problem," I say as I collect his paperwork and begin to focus back on the other folks.

What style was Ray? ______________________________

The Answers to Our Quiz

Did you take a guess at what style each person was in these four stories? Let's see how well you did.

Here are the answers:

Story 1 - Nurturer

Story 2 - Promoter

Story 3 - Examiner

Story 4 - Go-Getter

How many did you get right? __________

In reading the four stories about the different styles, can you see how easy it can be to identify someone, adapt to their style, help them feel comfortable and make them feel good at the same time?

To help you better understand the four styles, here is a list of character traits for each.

Go-Getters

- Driven
- Bold
- Opinionated
- Decisive
- Direct
- Strong desire to win
- Strong desire to lead
- Likes to be in charge
- Loves control
- Goal-oriented
- Has a "get it done now" attitude

Promoters

- Energetic
- Outgoing
- Fun-loving
- Positive

Promoters *Cont.*

- Talkative
- Loves recognition
- Dislikes details
- Loves to be the center of attention
- Enjoys simple uncomplicated things
- Tends to have a large social network

Nurturers

- Patient
- Helpful
- Understanding
- Reserved
- Careful
- Pleasing
- Sentimental
- Have a difficult time saying "no"
- Have deep relationships
- Are focused on helping others

Examiners

- Effective
- Efficient
- Thorough
- Research-oriented
- Avoids risks
- Loyal
- Knowledge-seeking
- Analyze everything
- May take a long time to develop trust
- Makes calculated decisions
- Enjoys strategies and processes

This is a short list of characteristics for each style. As we continue to deepen your understanding of the four styles, we will be giving you more and more information that will be useful, productive, simple and helpful.

Okay, look at that last sentence. We used four words that keyed into the four behavioral styles: useful, productive, simple and helpful. Do you see how you can include all four styles' language into one sentence? More on language later in the book.

Practice Identifying Behavioral Styles

Before we move to the next chapter, here's a way for you to be more effective if you want to begin practicing this information!

1. Find yourself a buddy to work with, maybe someone who is reading this book as well or has been to the Room Full of Referrals® program.
2. Make sure that you understand each other's behavioral style.
3. Select a networking function to attend.
4. While attending the function, meet just two to four people *separately*.
5. Then, before the function ends, make sure to introduce your buddy to those same two to four people.
6. After the function, describe what behavioral style you thought they were and see if your buddy agrees and why.
7. Remember, you have the ability to make people feel honored and respected with this information. Do your best to implement that with each person you come in contact with. Do not be fake or insincere.
8. Finally, keep in mind what Ivan often says: "Networking is about helping others as a way of growing your business." This is the gold standard of effective networking… so always look to help others first!

Now that you have a deeper knowledge of the four styles, let's move on to understanding what we call blends.

CHAPTER 5
Understanding Blends of the Behavioral Styles

All of us have some amount of each behavioral style within us in varying degrees of intensity. Some of us may have very, very small amounts of one or more of them with one style being very dominant. But, nonetheless, they're all still there.

The **blend** that you are demonstrates what makes you different from the other Nurturers, Go-Getters, Examiners or Promoters out there. Can you imagine a world where we were all only one style? How incredibly mundane and boring that would be. Our blend makes us unique, intriguing and unpredictable.

Blends can also make it more difficult to figure out someone else's most dominant behavioral style. When we can see multiple descriptors of a person's behavior, we have to ask more questions to decipher what their most dominant style could be. Some people have two styles that are maxed out, meaning the intensity of each is very high and around the same level.

Therefore, if you are trying to figure out someone who is maxed out in their top two styles, it could be difficult to say they have one dominant style. We want you to know that about 75% of the world has two styles over the average line.

If you can speak to someone in one of their top two styles, they will feel pretty darn comfortable with you! – Dawn

---

Tony Discusses His Blend

My blended style is Go-Getter/Promoter. When I have deadlines or need extra focus, my Go-Getter comes into play. Any phone calls I get while in my Go-Getter mode, I answer, "What?" My close colleagues, friends and family then know to keep the conversation short.

When I'm more relaxed and caught up on things, I'm in my Promoter mode. I may then answer the phone, "Tony's Pizzeria.

What toppings do you want?" Then, my close colleagues, friends and family know they can be more playful and longer-winded in their conversation.

Also, at my office desk, I tend to be more in my Go-Getter role. But on stage as a speaker, I'm definitely more in my Promoter style.

In referral marketing, where we deal with a lot of business owners, entrepreneurs and 100% commission type of people, there are a few blends that we encounter on a regular basis. We will describe some of them now.

Go-Getter/Promoters

Individuals who have these two styles are very prevalent in the networking scene. Their Go-Getter tends to be just a bit higher than the Promoter. At networking functions, they lead the conversations focused around business until they are satisfied that they accomplished what they needed to. Then they will stick around and have some fun with their friends.

They are business owners because they do not enjoy working for someone else. They network often because they love to meet people and feel that building relationships is way more fun than sitting behind the desk. They are easily noticed for their fast pace and ability to get things done while having a good time.

Promoter/Go-Getters

This blend is the same as above, but these people simply lead with their Promoter side. They will be more casual in their introduction and have a bit of energy. But they'll be more concerned about getting to know you and seeing if you are a cool person to hang out with or not. The business opportunities may come, but only after they feel you are a positive, enjoyable person.

Go-Getter/Nurturers

This blend is very interesting. A Go-Getter/Nurturer will lead with their Go-Getter style and have an intense need to help others. We actually have several Referral For Life® clients with this blend, and their intense opposite styles in action is an experience to watch.

They have an intense drive and desire to achieve but also a huge propensity to make sure others feel okay. They are constantly pulled between the fast pace they want to move in and the need to consider other's feelings and slow things down. They also battle with themselves because they know what must get accomplished, but if it doesn't feel right, it is very difficult to move forward.

The difference between task and people orientation is a bumpy road. It's a challenge to be assertive and cautious in the same step. Yet, one of Dawn's Go-Getter/Nurturer clients, a mortgage broker, actually doubled her income in just two years. And this was during 2009-2011... one of the worst economies ever! The strong desire to achieve a six-figure income and truly help her clients was an incredibly successful blend!

We Reveal *Our* Styles

Here is the perfect place to share with you what our styles are. Let's see if you can figure it out first! Before you read on take a guess at our behavioral style based only on the few stories we have told you so far.

Tony ______________________________

Ivan ______________________________

Dawn ______________________________

Ready for the answer? Our styles are the same. All three of us are Go-Getter first, then Promoter.

Throughout the rest of the book keep our style in mind, especially when we tell our individual stories. See if you can figure out our reactions, or how we had to adapt within the story, too!

CHAPTER 6
Top 10 Referral Marketing Basics

It has been said before that you should never assume anything because when you assume... well, we bet you know the rest of the phrase. So, we want to verify that we are all on the same page as far as referral marketing goes. That way, when we get into the different styles and how to treat them in different parts of your relationships, we'll all be talking about the same thing.

First of all, if you have not read *The World's Best Known Marketing Secret: Building Your Business by Referral*, then that book is a must-read. It's by Ivan and Mike Macedonio, president of the Referral Institute, two men who have created incredible success in referral marketing, not only for themselves but for thousands of business people. This book clearly defines the steps you will need to develop a referral marketing plan. What we will do for you here is give you some basics. If you need more direction or help, please purchase the book above as soon as possible or schedule a consultation with your local Referral Institute franchise owner. (Visit www.referralinstitute.com, then click on Regional Headquarters.)

By the way, even if you think you already know the basics *do not skip* this section.

Basics are for everyone; you must do them. You cannot skip these steps or you will forever wonder why you're not getting the results you're looking for!

A Story from Ivan: Wind Sprints

I learned an important lesson about the *fundamentals* of success while playing football many years ago. We had a fairly good team my junior year of high school. Most of the team was juniors. The following year the team had mostly seniors, and we had some pretty high expectations for the season. A situation like this can make one over-confident, and that's exactly how we were the beginning of my senior year.

When the season started, we experienced that brutal "rite of passage" for all football teams known as "Hell Week." It's called "Hell Week" for a very good reason; the conditioning that a team is put through is pure hell. The team does very little other than drills and exercises. I'm talking about isometric exercises, wind sprints (you know, those short-distance sprints as fast as you can possibly run), hitting bags, tackling dummies, running in place and hitting the ground on command, more wind sprints, running up and down stadium steps, hitting the sled (while the fattest coaches known to man are standing on them yelling at you) and did I mention wind sprints? Lots and lots of wind sprints!

We were doing so many drills, we never even saw a football (except when they were thrown at the backsides of some of the slower players)!

We knew we were going to be a good team, and we felt we didn't need to go through all this nonsense. We wanted to play ball, not run around the field, hit bags and do wind sprints! So, we had a little rebellion. We decided to pull our coach aside after a practice and tell him, "Coach, we don't want to do wind sprints anymore – we want to play ball!"

From my experience, coaches generally have two answers for anything they don't like. The first is, "NO!" and the second is, "What part of NO don't you understand?"

Imagine our surprise when he said, "Okay, I'll make you a deal, if you get here an hour early tomorrow morning for a little bus ride, I'll let you drop the conditioning program."

It took us all of about two seconds to say, "Road trip and no wind sprints – we're there coach!"

We were there early, and rode a bus with the coach to Cal State University - Fullerton. At that time, the university stadium was one of the practice fields for the Los Angeles Rams! When we realized we were going to see a Rams' practice, we were stoked!

We were in awe. It's one thing to be in a football stadium looking down at the field. But, it's something completely different to be on the field looking up. Even though it was the same size field as the one back home, it felt gigantic! If that wasn't enough, the Rams started to come onto the field.

If you've never seen professional football players up close and personal, let me tell you – these men are huge. When they are suited up, they are absolutely gigantic! Imagine a door frame with a football helmet. These guys had one eye in the middle of their head and hair on their teeth – they were frightening to stand next to.

We watched as our heroes stepped onto the field. We watched in total awe as they lumbered out onto the grass and, for the next two hours, did wind sprints! Yes, that's right – wind sprints. They were out there tackling dummies, hitting bags, running in place, attacking the sled (they had their own really fat coaches on the top yelling at them) and did I mention wind sprints, lots and lots of wind sprints. The truly amazing thing was that they were not only doing the same conditioning exercises, they were doing these exercises in the exact same order we were doing them.

When we returned to campus, the coach took us out and put us in a big semi-circle in the parking lot. Here, this football coach from this fairly small, lower-middle class high school said to us:

"Boys, it doesn't matter if you're talking about Pop Warner Football, high school football, college football, professional football or life. If you do not learn to execute the fundamentals flawlessly, you will never be a champion on or off the field. It doesn't matter if you are talking about football, school or work. When you leave this school and go on to college, you must learn the fundamentals and do the drills that will make you successful in your continuing education.

"When you go on to your professions and careers, you will see that there are fundamentals that you must learn in order to be a champion in that profession. Only those of you who are willing to develop the physical and mental conditioning necessary to execute these fundamentals will ever succeed. This is something you must choose. I can't choose it for you."

It took about 10 seconds for me and the 39 other young men on the team to *enthusiastically* choose to do… wind sprints.

We had a great season. But, more importantly, we learned an incredible life lesson. Success comes to those who execute the fundamentals flawlessly. It comes to those who work hard on the "right things." It comes to those who drill and learn and drill some more. ***It comes to those of us who, day in and day out, are willing to do the wind sprints necessary to succeed.***

Obviously, that story shows why it's necessary to not only know the basics but constantly practice them, too. The list below will get you started on some of the basic referral marketing skills. Start those drills.

The Top Ten Referral Marketing Basics

1. **Belong to three different networks:**
   - **A service network** like the Rotary Club, for example. Service clubs are devised for just that, to provide service to an organization. Your main reason for joining a service club would not be to gain business. Most people truly believe in what the organization is doing and have a passion for it. While your main goal is to serve the community or organization, you will also be building relationships and, yes, business may come to through this group. However, it should not be your main reason for joining.
   - **A social network,** like a Chamber of Commerce. Social networks provide a way for you to meet a larger amount of people at one time. There are less restrictions with this group,

and they mainly do large mixers. A key benefit to the social networks is you can meet people who would be good referrals for your referral sources. Having a large sphere of influence is important in your being able to give lots of referrals on a regular basis.

- **A strong contact network,** like BNI. Strong contact networks like BNI provide exclusivity. For example, only one person per profession is allowed to be a part of the group. They also incorporate more structure and commitment from their members, which in turn greatly increases the amount of loyalty and participation. These groups are designed to gain referral business. The key is to only belong to one of these types of groups to ensure follow-through, commitment and loyalty.[4]

When you create a strong referral network, you'll want to be able to give lots of referrals to them as well. You'll need a wide sphere of influence within which you have substantial credibility, so as they need things in their life, you can refer them. Mike Macedonio states, "It is not just the breadth of the relationships that you have, it's the breadth and the depth of relationships that are the most important." Being involved in three different networks will give you breadth - all you have to do is create the depth!

We are guessing that is why you are reading this book. So you can understand behavioral styles at a higher level and enjoy the fruits of deepening your relationships faster!

2. **Give referrals to others using behavioral styles**

   Giving referrals is not always an easy task. However, if you are using behavioral styles when giving referrals, we can guarantee you that your closing ratio of actually gaining the referral will go up dramatically.

[4] For more detailed information on these three networks, please read Chapter 17 in *The World's Best known Marketing Secret* by Dr. Ivan Misner and Mike Macedonio

A Story from Dawn: A Total Remodel

A girlfriend and I were at my home one evening having a glass of wine. She told me I needed to knock down the wall between my kitchen and dining room in order to "open it up." I could put some bar stools around a granite counter to make it more of an entertaining area where people could hang out instead of always standing in the kitchen. People could even sit at the dining room table and still feel part of the conversation because it would be so much more open. Then she told me she knew a contractor and would have him give me a call on Friday. WHOA! Hold on! Wait one stinking minute.

First of all, no contractor had better call me on Friday. Secondly, who says I even want to take down this wall. Lastly, I haven't heard anyone who comes over complain about standing around in my kitchen! Who did she think she was telling me what I should do, spending my money like it was hers and basically shoving this idea down my throat?

Okay, okay, I know my style is coming on pretty strong right now, but do you think she was treating me the way that I want to be treated? No way! The ironic part is she was trying to help me and help the contractor. Her heart was doing the right thing, but her mouth and her actions were not in sync with mine. All she had to do was change her behavioral style to adapt to mine, make me feel good about the idea, and she could have helped two people at once.

What if instead she said this: "Hey Dawn, how long are you going to stay here?"

"Maybe three to five years."

"Are you happy with the house?"

"Yeah, pretty much."

"Pretty much? Would you change anything if you could?"

"Well, I entertain a lot, so, of course, a bigger kitchen would be nice. It's just so small. I wish I had some bar stools so people could sit down but still be in the mix of things." "Well, what would that look like?"

"I don't know, maybe if this wall here was just a half-wall, it would open it up to the dining room, let in tons of light. I think it would make it look so much bigger in here, don't you think?"

She could then say, "Sure. Have you looked into what that might cost?"

"No, I am just thinking about this now. I have no idea if this is a load-bearing wall or not, so I guess I would have to have someone come in and take a look at it and get a quote. Do you know anyone?"

Do you see how if she'd gone about generating the referral in a way that intrigued my behavioral style, then she would have been able to get the referral for her contractor. I eventually did hire someone to do the work.

So, what were my friend's biggest mistakes?

- Telling me what I should do
- Making it her idea
- Basically saying my kitchen area stunk the way it was (insults are never a good way to go with any behavioral style)
- Shoving the contractor down my throat by telling me he would call me Friday
- Did I mention telling me what I should do???

Hopefully you get the picture here. When you are trying to generate a referral, you will want to do it by behavioral style for the best results.

3. **Train your referral network in what type of referrals you are looking for by speaking to their behavioral styles**

   In order to be successful at referral marketing, your referral team needs to be trained to find you the right referrals. It's your job to do that. If you decide to train someone, we hope you consider their behavioral style.

   What if, for example, an Examiner said to a Promoter, "Here are 17 pages of information on my products that you should know. Here is my website address. Please read that, too. And tomorrow I can give you my brochures and information packets to hand out to prospects."

   What do you think would happen? The Promoter is going to be totally turned off! He is going to have no desire to do any of that, and he is not going to refer people by handing them a brochure or information pack. Remember, you always bring your style to everything you do. Make sure to look at the style of the person in front of you and ask, "Am I treating them the way that they want to be treated?"

   Well, a Promoter would want to talk... yes, talk, about things - not read them! Preferably, they would want to be able to experience your product or service if possible! We will be sharing with you in Chapter 13 more about specific techniques for training your referral network based on their style.

4. **Be passionate about what you do and show others using their behavioral styles**

   Passionate people are referable! If you can showcase your passions to others they are much more inspired to help you.

5. **Compel others to want to help you**

   When we work with others within their behavioral styles, they simply find it very easy to work with us. When things are easy, we tend to do it more often, which is the exact result we are looking for from our referral sources. So compelling others to want to help us is all about making things very easy for them.

A Tip for Being Passionate from Dawn

When I am in front of an audience, I do a role-play, asking the whole crowd to ask me, "So, what do you do?"

As part of the role, I reply, "Oh, I, uh, have a graphic design business. It's okay. I mean it's a job, and we get by all right, I guess. Being a graphic designer, we have our good days and bad days just like anyone else."

YUCK! Would you be inspired to help me? Would you ever send me a referral? Most likely not!

What if I replied instead, "I have a growing graphic design business, and every day I get out of bed knowing I will make a huge impact on one of my clients as I help them develop and create their brand! I love knowing that I am part of propelling their business to the next level. It's exciting, creative and incredibly rewarding. I look forward to each and every new day."

Now, please make sure to not go overboard the other way and be too passionate or obnoxiously excited. The important part is to hear the enthusiasm, the love of the business and how you help people. That is so very important!

Sharing your passion by behavioral style is simply using the correct language with the person. You will learn each style's language in Chapter 10.

Have you ever gone to a networking function and said to yourself, "Oh, I hope so-and-so is not there. I really hope they don't ask me out to coffee or something… I just don't click with them."

When you are unable to click with someone, it's going to be very difficult to compel them to help you. Adaptability is crucial to your referral success, and, in many cases, it's simply identifying the other person's style and adapting your language and training techniques. Simple as that! Stay tuned because in Chapter 14 we'll show you how to do exactly that!

6. Build deep referral relationships

Many people have surface-level referral relationships. They know just enough about a referral source's business to get by. They don't actually know a lot about the person themselves. They tend to say vague things like: "They are really nice," "You'll like them, they are a good person", or "Well, if you just meet with them, I am sure you'll like them."

So, what are the key points to having a deep referral relationship? If you know the following points about a person and her business, you would have a pretty deep referral relationship:

- You believe they are an expert at what they do.
- You trust them to do a great job and take great care of your referred prospects.
- You have known each other for at least one year.
- You understand at least three major products or services within their business and feel comfortable explaining them to others.
- You know the names of their family members and have met them personally.
- You have both asked each other how you can help grow your respective businesses.
- You know at least five of their goals for the year, including personal and business goals.
- You could call them at 10 o'clock at night if you really needed something.
- You would not feel awkward asking them for help with either a personal or business challenge.
- You enjoy the time you spend together.
- You have regular appointments scheduled, both business and personal.

- You enjoy seeing them achieve further success.
- They are "top of mind" each and every day.
- You have open, honest talks about how you can help each other further.

You may be shocked at the level of personal knowledge required for a deep referral relationship, feeling that referrals should be all about business. We completely disagree. It takes a lot to develop this type of relationship, and our hope is that you'll make the effort with someone you truly like, have the desire to help and want to spend time with!

7. Spend your precious business networking time using behavioral style skills

Many folks fail to use behavioral styles while at networking functions. It's a mistake because behavioral styles allow you to make such a great first impression. People simply feel more comfortable with you, and therefore will spend more time with you. In turn, this allows you to decide if this is someone you would like to engage with after the event. Your time is precious… use it wisely.

8. Use behavioral styles every day in your relationships

At first, this is not going to come naturally. You'll want to practice. It really is like learning a new language, only you have to learn four new ones! When you apply this to all of your relationships and practice every day… that's how you become unconsciously competent with this strategy. Remember to serve others and come from the right heart, and you will do great.

9. Track and reward your referral network by behavioral style

When you begin to track your referral results, you will also want to have a reward system. This system should be based on three things: 1) the amount of referrals given, 2) the amount of closed business generated and 3) of course behavioral style. The four styles appreciate different types of rewards. We are not talking about humongous presents or anything like that. In many cases, it is something very simple and fairly small that the styles are looking for.

Let's begin with what you could be tracking. There are several items we want to encourage you to track on a regular basis. Such as:

- Who referred you?
- What level of relationship do you have with them?
- What is the name of the prospect?
- When did you connect with the prospect?
- Was an appointment set up and when?
- Did the prospect choose to buy your services? If so, how much did they spend?
- How long did it take them to decide to purchase?
- Are they a recurring client?
- Have they referred you any new prospects?
- Did you send the "giver" of the referral a thank you card just for sending you a referral?
- Did you send the "giver" of the referral a small gift of sorts if the referral closed or didn't close?
- If so, what was the gift?

What if these items were in an Excel spreadsheet, and you could begin tracking your referral revenue today?! Well, you are in luck. If you go to www.RoomFullofReferrals.com and look at the downloadable section, we have an example form you can use to get started with titled Referral Institute Tracking & Rewarding Spreadsheet.

Now, for those of you who are a bit more advanced, the Referral Institute also has a complete referral marketing tracking system called Relate2Profit.[5]

This system allows you to enter in your referral sources, track activities with them, pull hundreds of reports, and much more. By tracking your referral marketing activities with Relate2Profit, you can adjust your strategy to focus on the specific techniques to improve your level of relationships, closing ratio, your lead time to generating more profit for your business and ultimately have a clear comprehension as to whom you should be spending more or less time with each and every week.

Check with your local Referral Institute franchise owner or use the code in the footnote below to receive a special offer.

Tracking is a huge part of any business. Tracking the basics is great. By seeing the results your referral sources have had on your business revenue and then rewarding them in their style, you continue to motivate them properly and will continue to evoke the best from them!

For example, Go-Getters tend to like "nice" things. So, don't be cheap or give something they would re-gift. They also like things that are engraved with their name, something exclusive or anything that implies VIP.

Promoters like things they can do with other people, like go to a concert or dinner. You also want to wrap their gift, and if you find out their favorite color, they will already love it without even knowing what's inside! They love tearing open wrapping paper, and it's fun to watch them!

Nurturers tend to simply want acknowledgement and appreciation. A simple, but a very personal thank you card is typically sufficient for Nurturers. If you go the extra mile and there is a picture on the card of something *they* love, you will have shown them you truly listen to them. Also, if they have a charity and you give a donation in their name, they will be forever thankful. Be sure not to get an overly extravagant gift, as in many cases the Nurturer will feel you have gone overboard and feel a need (even guilt) to reciprocate.

Examiners really appreciate useful gifts. Something practical like a gift card so they can pick out what they really need versus receiving a gift they don't like. Practical and useful is the way, like an office supply gift card, a gas gift card… that makes sense to them.

10. **Read *The World's Best-Known Marketing Secret – Building Your Business by Referral* Cover to Cover after You Have Completed this Book**

    This is the one step you cannot afford to miss. This book gives incredible detail about how to develop a referral marketing plan. It has tons of simple tips and techniques you can implement easily into your business right away! It will definitely provide you some wonderful ideas about how to give more referrals, and you will be shocked at how much more efficient you will be in your marketing efforts!

    If you can't tell by now, we are pretty passionate about having you implement this behavioral style material into every aspect of your referral marketing efforts! We believe it is the icing on the cake!

[5] Relate2Profit is a web-based, referral tracking application designed by ZINCASTLE Software Systems, who has been a strategic alliance with the Referral Institute for more than seven years. For more information, please go to: www.Relate2Profit.com. Use the Referral Code **Room-Full** to receive a special offer.

CHAPTER 7
Strengths and Challenges of Each Behavioral Style

The wonderful part about behavioral styles is that each one of them has multiple strengths while networking. Some are much more conducive to large networking functions, while others are better suited for more one–to-one conversations. Yet all of them have their strengths – which implies that each has its own specific challenges, too. In this chapter, we will describe these strengths and challenges for you.

Remember that you have all four styles within you in varying degrees of intensity. Many of you will read one style and say, "Yep, that's me!" Then you will read another style's strengths and say, "Wait, that's me too." While reading the lists of strengths you may feel as if you have some of two different styles. You could be completely correct.

You were given specific gifts and talents – use them! You can always hire people to do what you are not great at!

We suggest that when you read through your most dominant style, that you check off the strengths you know to be true about you. Then see if another style's strengths also relate to you. If so, you may have a high intensity on that second style as well. You can choose to do the same with your challenges by simply placing a check mark next to it.

Now, the three of us have one very strong belief in common. We believe that when people focus on their strengths great things happen. You were given specific gifts and talents – use them! You can always hire people to do what you are not great at! In fact, those things you are not great at are probably their strengths! It's a win-win situation!

A Story from Dawn: My Opposite

My administrative assistant, Dorothy Bacon, is phenomenal. Her strengths are the exact opposite of mine. She excels at details, data entry, processes, structure, thoroughness and much more.

When my business got to the point of way too much for me to handle, I knew I wanted to hire an Examiner to take care of all of the above for me. She has been working for me for 10 years, and it is a match made in heaven. I realized my talents were not in those areas. Even if I tried really hard to accomplish them, I wouldn't be very happy. I would constantly be trying to work on things that I am weak at instead of breezing through the day working on things I am great at!

We will give you some tips at the end of this chapter to encourage you to overcome your challenges. There is a big secret that we will share with you that will make dealing with your challenge areas very simple.

Let's start with the *Go-Getters!*

Strengths while Networking – Go-Getters tend to...

- Stay very focused on their desired outcome.
- Have the ability to keep their conversations centered around business.
- Attend functions with a result or goal in mind.
- Make things happen, versus wait for them to happen.
- Introduce themselves to others with no fear of rejection.
- Seek out the most successful people in the room.
- Make quick decisions whether the person they are talking to is a good fit.
- Have an easy time being specific – which can lead to quicker referrals.
- Exude confidence, which will help them be perceived as an expert.

- They are willing to take risks.
- They enjoy being in charge.
- They have a solutions-focused attitude.

Knowing that sometimes a strength can also be a challenge, we will give you some new challenges and then expand upon why some of the strengths above are also challenges.

Go-Getters

Challenges while Networking – Go-Getters tend to...

- Not let people get very close to them.
- Get impatient easily.
- Have an intense need for quick results.
- Ask for too much too soon.
- Be seen as arrogant.
- Be seen as all business when not sharing any personal information.
- Sometimes be too focused on goals and not focused enough on the relationship.

Promoters

Strengths while Networking – Promoters tend to...

- Attract people with their energy.
- Love meeting new people.
- Use their smile to be very approachable.
- Make others feel good by encouraging them.
- Know lots of people at the event.
- Be okay with being the life of the party.
- Be great communicators.
- Be very spontaneous.

- Be okay with changes.
- Like to work in group situations.
- Are up for new ideas and ways of doing things.
- Love adventure.
- Use their enthusiasm and "positivity."

Promoters

Challenges while Networking – Promoters tend to...

- Not get down to business fast enough.
- Have a tendency to talk about themselves a lot.
- Be known for telling long stories.
- Be seen as distracted as they see all their friends at an event.
- Be more concerned with having fun than gaining business.
- Be viewed as not very focused.
- Be known for spreading themselves too thin.

Nurturers

Strengths while Networking – Nurturers tend to...

- Make others feel very comfortable.
- Take care of folks who are unsure.
- Have deep meaningful relationships with people at the event.
- Be great listeners.
- Be passionate about what the event stands for or they wouldn't be there.
- Spend quality time with people.
- Be willing to share personal information easily.
- Be a little bit reserved.

- Want to deepen current relationships versus trying to meet 20 people in one night.
- Be okay with not being in the spotlight.
- Be mostly concerned with finding others they can help in some way.

Nurturers

Challenges while Networking – Nurturers tend to...

- Not ask for things.
- Rarely brag about themselves and their success.
- Not be concerned with dressing to impress others (which could be a turn off for the Go-Getters).
- Spend time asking what others might see as questions that are too personal.
- Focus on all personal information rather than a combination of both personal and business.
- Be typically unwilling to move quickly into a business relationship.
- Say "yes" to many things that do not generate business results for them but often do for others.

Examiners

We may need to explain a few things with this style before giving you a list of strengths. Many of the Examiners that we deal with as entrepreneurs will often state, "I do not enjoy networking, but I know it is a necessity for my business."

This is something that we find stays very true to their actual style. Examiners, being slower-paced and task-oriented type of folks, tend to take a while to develop relationships. And even when they do, many of the relationships are business-oriented or have something to do with completing specific tasks in their lives. Though we can still give you a list of the strengths of Examiners while networking, please know that it is something they may do out of necessity and not enjoyment.

Examiners

Strengths while Networking – Examiners tend to…

- Attend networking functions with a goal or intent clearly-defined.
- Be focused on one-to-one conversations.
- Ask lots of questions about your business.
- Complete their goal and then leave the event.
- Understand lots of different businesses, so they are good at conversing about many industries.

Examiners

Challenges while Networking – Examiners tend to…

- Not enjoy meeting lots of strangers at events.
- Only stay for a short time, unless they have a job to do at the function.
- Only talk about business and not personal information.
- Want to blend into the crowd instead of standing out.
- Speak in factual or procedural language instead of emotion-based words that will attract the Nurturers and Promoters.
- Show an awkward side of themselves as they simply appear nervous or "closed."

CHAPTER 8
Areas to Improve on with Each Behavioral Style

In this chapter, the goal is to show you exactly how to improve your communication with each style while networking. This is such a crucial part to developing relationships of the best quality. It may seem simple. But if it were possible to take away all of the silly things that annoy people in relationships and leave all of the things they love, would you have higher-quality relationships? Of course!

The question is, are you willing to make changes, improve and think more about others in order to have that? If so, pay close attention to this chapter. Make sure to take small steps – don't try to change everything at once, or you will go crazy! At the end of this chapter we have included a worksheet that will allow you to decide who you will begin making small changes with.

Here is how this chapter works: We will begin by highlighting one style and then showing what improvements people with that style can make to better deal with people of all four styles while networking. We'll also explain how to develop a deeper, more meaningful relationship. Yes, you can improve your relationship with people of the same style as yours.

You may feel as though you want to skip directly to your own style. We would like to discourage you from doing that. Remember, knowing more about all four styles is the ultimate goal here. Yes, you always bring your style to the table first. But we promise you, you will learn plenty by reading the other styles too.

Remember that we are a blend of all four styles in varying degrees of intensity. It is in the different degrees of intensity where you will need more finesse. This is what can catapult you into "unconscious competence" with these strategies.

Areas of Improvement for Go-Getters

Let's begin with the Go-Getters. (By the way, do you know why we start with them? They're impatient and love to be first – and, of course, they believe they are the most important anyway, so why not begin everything with them! Just kidding Go-Getters… well, not really. If you are honest with yourselves, we're sure you are saying, "Yeah, and so what?!")

Areas that Go-Getters can improve with other Go-Getters while networking

- Allow them to talk about themselves more than you talk about yourself.
- Ask them about their achievements – don't declare yours first.
- Don't "one up them." You two will be there all night "one upping" each other.
- Decide quickly how you can make them look good.
- Choose a simple way to help them as soon as possible – get them a result from meeting you.
- Show them why they want to continue talking to you.

Deepening a current relationship, Go-Getter to Go-Getter

- Once appropriate, "break their shell." Go-Getters tend to not let people get very close to them. In many cases, they have a huge impenetrable wall around them. If people get too close to them, they might see their inadequacies or weaknesses, and that is just not right. Once you feel you have a high level of trust, find a way to get closer to them. Ask for more time together to get even more strategic. Figure out their true passion and help them with it. Let them know they can count on you at any time.
- Find a way to make the relationship more personal. Remember, Go-Getters tend to keep things to business. When you can make the relationship more personal, they begin to allow you into their life, which will help you get closer.
- It may sound crazy but be willing to share with them first the silly mistakes you have made as a Go-Getter. It can bring

down their guard a bit… just don't go overboard and declare every mistake ever made. (Oh wait, that wouldn't happen as most of you as Go-Getters will have a hard enough time just declaring even small mistakes!) We promise it works. It makes you human. Living up to such incredibly high standards all of the time does get exhausting!

- Be open to constantly discussing new, more strategic ways of working together. Brainstorm with each other. Please note that in brainstorming there are no bad ideas; you just throw out everything you can think of and truly go for it! Then you can select what is really possible and set a plan to make it work.
- Constantly have them thinking about you as someone long-term in their life. Phrases like, "In the next five years if we could accomplish X, we would kill the competition out there!" will show them they are not spending this time and working with you so closely for no reason. This is going to be a powerful relationship. Remember, everything they do has to be "worth it!"

Areas that a Go-Getter can improve on with a Promoter while networking

- Go-Getters, lighten up! Skip some of the business chat and ask them, "What do you do when you are not working?" or "What do you do for fun?" Find out information about them other than business.
- Stay very positive no matter what you are talking about! Forget most of the stats or technical stuff you could talk about and let them talk about themselves. Remember they are people-oriented, so you can ask them, "What other networks do you belong to?" or "Who do you know in that network?"
- Keep your energy high, positive and lighthearted – not too serious.

- Stay focused on getting them to talk about themselves, forget about being the center of attention yourself and let the Promoter stand out. They will leave the conversation feeling fantastic and wanting to hang out with you more!

Deepening a current relationship as a Go-Getter with a Promoter

- Ask yourself, "What was the last fun thing I did with my Promoter referral source?" Keeping the business relationship fun and personal is crucial to long-term success. When was the last time the two of you laughed together? These are serious questions to ask. If the Promoter isn't having fun in the relationship, they will be inspired to help someone else they do have fun with!
- Are you recognizing the Promoter for the work and effort they put into referring you? As Tony often states, a "well done" typically comes from a Go-Getter only if they are ordering a steak! Go-Getters tend to expect things from others versus continue to recognize their efforts. You will learn more about motivating other styles in Chapter 9.
- Keep the two of you on track and have fun doing it. Pressure does not work with Promoters. You have to find a creative, positive way to keep track of referrals or the results you are looking for from the relationship. If the relationship develops too much pressure the Promoter will be gone. Pressure is not fun, not positive (in their mind) and definitely not something they enjoy being involved with.

Areas a Go-Getter can improve on with a Nurturer while networking

- Be patient! Be okay with spending several more minutes with them and do not rush your conversation. Give them some quality time.
- Be present with them. Don't drift off while they explain something; be present in the conversation. If they do not feel important enough, you have lost the opportunity.

- Be willing to ask them business and personal questions. Some of our favorites are "Have you lived here long?", "Does your family live close?" or "Can you share with me what you love about your work?" These questions can start many quality conversations and help you hit the personal aspect you're looking for.
- Watch your intensity as a Go-Getter. Nurturers won't jump at things; they have to be fully comfortable with their next step. So, no pressure. Show your intent of creating a long-term relationship with them. Be okay with going a bit slower to make sure they trust you fully. Use phrases such as, "It would be really nice to spend some more time with you to learn more about you and how you truly help others." Remember, Nurturers are great listeners, which means they can give great quality referrals if they trust you deeply enough!

Deepening a current relationship as a Go-Getter with Nurturers

- Give them more time. It shows them that you value the relationship, as they understand how valuable your time is. When you share time with them they know they are important to you. Go to lunch with them, or better yet, have them to dinner at your home. Let them into your life!
- Get personal. Know as much as you can about them, their family, their desires, their passions, what and who they love. Yes, everything personal you can think of! You will just have to trust me on this one, Go-Getter. Just do it!
- Share with them the "what ifs," such as: "What if our businesses looked like X?" or "What if you and I could actually do X together?" These phrases allow them to think about the possibilities without bringing on pressure. Now, you cannot get their answer and then say, "Okay, let's have that done by next week!" That is pressure.

  Just discuss and share and then let it linger on in the conversation: "Yeah, that would be nice someday." When you want them to act on something give them plenty of time to think about it and what their actions would look like. Nurturers must feel comfortable before moving forward.

Areas a Go-Getter can improve on with an Examiner while networking

- Make sure to not rush the conversation. Ask them a lot of questions about their business and definitely stick to business. You want to get great at keeping the conversation natural – not like an interrogation. Sometimes when Go-Getters ask a lot of questions, it can become defensive. People don't know why you are asking so many questions. Make it conversational, not combative.
- Only speak of one main achievement unless directly asked. Examiners take a while to make their mind up about someone and if you brag about yourself too much up front, it will turn them off. Lighten the intensity of any achievement and stay humble.
- Be okay with asking them what they are looking to accomplish at the event. Examiners, like you, came with a clear goal or intent in mind.

Deepening a current relationship as a Go-Getter with an Examiner

- Be consistent in the relationship. Examiners must understand the procedure of the relationship, what their expectations are, time commitments, etc. Long-term thinking is crucial with Examiners. They want to know you will be around long term or the investment of time with you may not provide a good return.
- Examiners – like Nurturers – do not accept change easily, so give them plenty of notice on anything new. Use phrases such as, "I have been thinking about X. I'm not sure what my next step will be just yet, but thought you may want to know."

  In many cases when we have used this technique, the Examiner has actually done some research on our behalf and helped us with the process. They've taken the time to help us identify the next steps or even put us in touch with an expert who would know what to do next.

- Keep records and details on the amount of referrals being passed between each other. It is not that the dollar amount has to be equal; it is more important that the relationship is successful in the expectations set by each side.

Go-Getters, now that you know what areas you can improve on, can you see how easy it would be to increase the results you're currently receiving from your networking efforts and your referral relationships? By simply making a few adjustments, you will have dramatic changes that can substantially increase the bottom line in your business. Best of luck... wait, you don't believe in luck, you believe in making it happen, so... make it happen!

Areas of Improvement for Promoters

Promoters, this next section is 100% for you! This is exactly what you will need to take simple steps that allow people to love you even more than they do right now! By the time you finish reading this section you will have many people in mind for better and deeper relationships. We know you can do this! Remember, there is going to be a worksheet at the end of this chapter to help you write down some of the next steps to take. So pay close attention. Enjoy!

Areas a Promoter can improve on with Go-Getters while networking

- Be extremely focused in your conversation. Even if friends are arriving, stay in full eye contact with the Go-Getters. This will show them you are not distracted easily, as they want your undivided attention.
- Be okay with getting directly down to business. Keep the majority of the conversation centered on them. Ask about their achievements in business and even what their area of expertise is.
- Keep your sentences or stories short. Go-Getters don't need

a lot of details to make decisions. They are already trying to finish your sentences!

- Do not take up too much of their time. Make sure they see the value in getting to know you better - what's in it for them? They must know that in order to book an appointment with you.

Deepening a current relationship as a Promoter with Go-Getters

- If you used to have a great relationship with a Go-Getter check to see where you may have gotten distracted. Ensure the Go-Getter you are back on track, focused and ready to go to work. Ask them what their next goal is and see how you can help. Show them results of your referral efforts quickly. Use your strength of connecting them with someone!
- Show them on your calendar when you plan on working on their behalf. This will show focus and clarity of your efforts.
- When you accomplish something for them, make sure they know about it. Email them or phone them the results *immediately* – don't wait until your next meeting.
- Always start with business. If there is time afterward, ask them personal questions. Make sure to get the business done first.

Areas a Promoter can improve on with other Promoters while networking

- Allow the other Promoter to have the spotlight in the conversation. Be the listener this time!
- Be your fun and energetic self, yet definitely ask a few business questions.
- Phrases such as, "We could have a blast working together if we just knew each other better!" work very well. They show the other Promoter you are business-oriented, yet able to have fun while working.
- Ask the other Promoter questions about their goals.

Deepening a current relationship as a Promoter with other Promoters

- Be the Promoter who stays focused when together.
- Be willing to "keep track" of successes so you can celebrate them together.
- Be creative and even set up bets or games for each other. It can make doing business together that much more fun!
- Ask how you can help them personally – many Promoters are overwhelmed and often need help but do not enjoy asking for it.
- Did we already mention celebrate successes together… this is truly important to deepening the relationship!

Areas a Promoter can improve on with Nurturers while networking

- Be careful about being too exuberant when first meeting someone.
- Allow them to speak more than you while in conversation.
- Ask meaningful questions about them and definitely include personal information.
- Be genuine and truly focused on your conversation with them.
- Keep a strong yet sincere form of eye contact with them.
- Let them know you are looking for meaningful long-term relationships.

Deepening a current relationship as a Promoter with a Nurturer

- Ask yourself when was the last time you sat down and truly focused on their needs?
- Make sure to spend quality time with them alone, not in large groups. This shows true interest in being with them.
- Figure out ways to make them feel important in your relationship.

- Give them lots of one-to-one verbal recognition.
- If you feel like they are not moving fast enough in the relationship, then there probably is not enough trust. To overcome this have more meaningful conversations with them and show them you are in the relationship for the long haul.

Areas a Promoter can improve on with Examiners while networking

- Be willing to ask lots and lots of questions about them. They will tend to give you short answers; be okay with it.
- When they begin explaining things in detail – keep listening! Paying attention will show your interest in them.
- Keep your conversation mainly focused on business.
- A great question to ask them is, "What are you looking to accomplish by being at this event tonight?" Then, see if you can help them do that.
- If you feel the need to connect an Examiner to another person at an event, please be sure to fully explain the reason why, so they understand the purpose of the introduction.

Deepening a current relationship as a Promoter with an Examiner

- Slow down and have a very specific meeting with them as to how they feel the relationship is progressing.
- Ask them, "What, if anything, could we do to improve upon this relationship?" Then see how they would like things to change and ask them to be specific.
- Ask them if they would be willing to track the referral results the two of you are creating in order to create a system to measure the results you are getting from working together. Then make sure you are getting them results!
- Remember that in referral marketing, Examiners are incredible at putting together systems. Once they accomplish that the referrals can flow in very easily for you. So, help

them to see what systems they might be able to put in place for you… and you may want to do the same for them!

Areas of Improvement for Nurturers

Nurturers, we would now like to share with you the ways that you can improve your relationships while networking. This section is devoted to helping you see where you can make others feel even better about new relationships and also take the current relationships you have and make them even more important to you.

You are wonderful at honoring others, and this section will simply take your skill set to another level of development. The worksheet at the end of this chapter will help you discover a few of the missing pieces you may want to incorporate while networking. In truth, it will help you to help others! We hope you like it!

Areas a Nurturer can improve on with Go-Getters while networking

- Dress to impress. Go-Getters are attracted to success and one thing they look at is the way someone looks. If you want to attract more Go-Getters to you, we suggest stepping up your business image.
- While in conversation with them, ask them very direct questions – they are okay with it!
- Ask them what they are looking to achieve in their business.
- Find out why they are at the function and see if you can help them gain the results they are looking for.
- Be sure to show off your best posture, best strong stance, be relational yet focused and determined and make sure they know why they need you!

Deepening a current relationship as a Nurturer with Go-Getters

- When meeting with them be fully-prepared. They like to work fast, so if you are unable to make a decision, simply say, "I will get back to you on that." Then do get back to them as soon as possible.

- Come to the meeting with objectives in mind or even an agenda, they will love it!
- Be willing to talk business first and then, if there is time, some chit-chat at the end.
- Think over possibilities before any meetings, so you are clear on what you would like to see accomplished and then simply state that. Again, they are okay with directness.
- Make sure to be deliberate and ask them for things as well. They will appreciate the fact that you are keeping them on their toes in the relationship!

Areas a Nurturer can improve on with Promoters while networking

- Smile a lot! Promoters are attracted to positive, happy people, so smiling can go a long way with them!
- Increase your energy level just a tad. They will like that.
- Maybe talk a bit more with your hands and be a bit animated – only if that works for you.
- Talk about personal things but, at some point, ask them, "What are you looking to do in your business this year?" Then listen, which you are very good at.
- Be sincerely interested in them and share how you think you might be able to help them.

Deepening a current relationship as a Nurturer with Promoters

- Keep any meetings moving at a quick pace. Meeting at different locations can make it interesting for them.
- Be aware that they may get off-track easily, and you will tend "go with them" because you like to listen to their needs. Be the one that keeps the meeting on track. As they enjoy being with you and they gain more business, you are creating value in the relationship.
- Be a connector for them! They are always connecting other people. Find out who they truly want to be connected to and then help them.

- Do as much as you can to make them famous within your network.
- Gain time with them alone. In big groups, they tend to be in "on mode," so when they can just be with you it is a bit more down to earth and relaxing for them… something they could use a bit more of in life.

Areas a Nurturer can improve on with other Nurturers while networking

- Get good at asking for permission to talk about business. See, Nurturer-to-Nurturer you may spend a great deal of time chatting about more personal items. Once you have the connection you are looking for simply say, "Would it be okay if we discussed our businesses a little bit?"
- If you feel you have a connection with a Nurturer, be sure to ask for the next meeting with them to develop the relationship. Don't assume they will ask you! Remember, asking is not one of the Nurturer's strengths!
- Please realize that your mannerisms, such as pace, hand gestures and tonality will probably be very comfortable for the two of you. That's why we didn't ask you to change or do anything differently.

Deepening a current relationship as a Nurturer with another Nurturer

- Ask for permission at the beginning of the relationship to be able to openly ask for what the two of you may need from each other. If you don't ask, you don't get.
- Set specific appointments for just getting together and meeting with others for business. This will keep the intention of the meetings clear.
- Do be involved in their personal life in some way.
- Be willing to have appointments scheduled out in advance because, as you know, Nurturers can over-extend

themselves in helping others and forget to book the business appointments they need to build their own referral relationships.

Areas a Nurturer can improve on with Examiners while networking

- Look at having a more structured conversation with an Examiner. It will make them feel incredibly comfortable.
- Understand that as you ask them questions, you may receive short answers. It's okay, keep asking questions until you really strike a chord with them, and they will begin to be more lengthy in their responses.
- Do keep your conversation focused on business.
- Ask direct questions.
- Ask them how you might be able to help them at the event. Typically, Examiners are not incredibly excited about being at a networking function. If your offer can help them achieve the task at hand, they will be most grateful.

Deepening a current relationship as a Nurturer with an Examiner

- Ask them, "What aspects of the relationship are they satisfied with?"
- Talk openly about the documented results you have gotten each other.
- Discuss new systems or processes you could put in place on each other's behalf.
- Be sure you have a full understanding of what their expectations are for the relationship moving forward.
- When appropriate, create a way to be involved in their personal life, too.

Areas of Improvement for Examiners

Examiners, this next section will describe a thorough and effective way for you to improve your relationships with each style. You can rest assured that these strategies will create the desired results for your referral marketing efforts. The worksheet at the end of this chapter will provide you with a road map to taking the next steps. Complete it, and you will find value.

Areas an Examiner can improve on with Go-Getters while networking

- Be willing to introduce yourself to them. Examiners tend to wait for others to introduce themselves. You doing it first it shows confidence, ambition and directness – which all Go-Getters love.
- When speaking with them speed up your pace of speech. Go-Getters are fast-paced and can get bored with conversations easily. When you appeal to this aspect, you will keep them engaged in the conversation that much easier.
- Keep the conversation focused on them and their business.
- Give them a specific reason as to why they should get to know you better. For example, a statement such as, "I have over 500 loyal clients," can really gain their attention.
- If your strategy is to attract more Go-Getters, then be sure to project the professional business image they will be attracted to.

Deepening a current relationship as an Examiner with a Go-Getter

- Because both Examiners and Go-Getters are task-oriented, it's likely things will stay focused on business only. Go deeper. Get involved in their personal lives in a way that makes you become closer.
- Have scheduled appointments with each other already set up. Go-Getters tend to have very intense schedules. Make sure you get your deserved time with them. Your ability to plan far in advance will help with this.
- If the Go-Getter gets a little behind on their objectives with you, do not be intimidated about asking them to recommit. They enjoy the challenge and will be able to handle "being called out."

- Go-Getters can make things happen pretty easily, but what you want from them is a structured system they will agree to working within consistently with you. This is another opportunity for you to show them how much easier a structured system is and how it can guarantee you both more results. When there are more results, they stay in relationships longer.

Areas an Examiner can improve on with Promoters while networking

- Energy and a big smile are key!
- Pace of speech should also be a bit faster with Promoters.
- Ask them tons of questions about themselves and be okay with them talking for a while.
- Be incredibly complimentary to them about any accomplishments they may share with you, and ask them questions like, "How did that feel?" You will see them light up!
- Keep all conversation very positive, upbeat and light. Don't be too intense right at the beginning.

Deepening a current relationship as an Examiner with a Promoter

- Keep it fun and interesting! Surprise them whenever you can.
- Offer to do worksheets/charts/Excel programs to track the goals or projects you are working on together… they will love you for it!
- Be the one who keeps them focused – they will thank you later.
- Be willing to open up to them more often. Allow them into your personal life in some way.
- Look at the time you spend together. If it is always business-focused, you will want to schedule some fun time, too!

- Listen carefully to their conversations, and they will tell you what their passions are. You may be able to schedule the fun around their passion!

Areas an Examiner can improve on with Nurturers while networking

- Be willing to talk about more personal items.
- Share with them more of who you are, how you got into business and why you love what you do rather than "what you do." This allows them to get to know you better.
- Try lengthening your sentences to sound more conversational. It will come across more genuine versus direct.
- Ask questions such as, "What do you love most about your business?" You are allowing them to tell you how they help people, which they love doing.

Deepening a current relationship as an Examiner with a Nurturer

- Ask yourself, "How much do I know about them personally?" If it's not a lot, then that is where you need to focus and be more deliberate.
- Spend time during any meetings with them talking about family, friends or activities they did recently. It shows you care.
- Get involved with a project or charity they might be passionate about. It takes your relationship past just business.
- Help them get better at asking you for more business, referrals, etc. Nurturers tend to not like to ask people for things. When you allow them or even encourage them to ask you for something, you are helping them deal with that issue.

Areas an Examiner can improve on with other Examiners while networking

- Encourage each other to share more personal information.
- Your tendency will be to enjoy talking to only each other for the majority of the event. Instead, deliberately choose to meet others and encourage each other to do so.
- Watch out for how opinionated you are on a subject when first meeting someone. Examiners tend to have strong stances on many subjects. Networking functions may not be the appropriate place to offer those opinions initially.
- Look at meeting more often at the start of a new relationship to move the process forward faster. You'll gain more effective relationships faster as well.

Deepening a current relationship as an Examiner with another Examiner

- Identify what processes or systems you have in place for each other and evaluate them on their success.
- Discuss new opportunities the two of you might have to increase your referral efforts together.
- When appropriate, make a conscious decision to open up and share more personal information with each other.
- Begin spending time together on a regular schedule and be sure to strategically schedule "personal time" too. We know that sounds very odd. Yet, it is ultimately necessary to have the most effective referral relationship.

We understand that no one is perfect, and you are not going to be able to implement all of this at your very next networking function. But it is something to work towards. Do you think if you knew this information 20 years ago that you would have some different relationships in your life today? We are sure you would!

We would like to have you document some of your next steps with the material you just learned. The worksheet you are about to go through is a simple yet effective way to gather some information and put it to great use in generating better quality relationships that will ultimately last longer than any you've ever had.

Areas of Improvement Worksheet

Where will you choose to begin improving your skills?

1. At networking events you typically wind up talking to:

2. You usually feel the most comfortable with which styles?

3. You feel the most uncomfortable with which styles?

4. Can all styles become excellent referrals sources for you?

5. Thinking about the different networks you belong to, write down the names of the members under the style you believe them to be in each network. Yes, you may be guessing right now, but it's okay.

	Go-Getters	Promoters	Nurturers	Examiners
BNI				
Chamber				
Rotary				
Prof. Assn.				
School				
Church				
Other				

Obviously, this is just a quick way to get you started on identifying the behavioral styles of the people that you currently know in your network. If you get stuck on guessing their style, at least go back and decide if they are fast-paced or slower-paced and people-oriented or task-oriented. This will help you begin to clarify their style.

Now, circle your top five relationships in each category. When you look back at the ways that you can deepen the relationship for your style, select a few conversations or things you can do.

Here is an example:

For the Chamber section, you have written down Susie. Susie is a Nurturer, and you are a Promoter. What can you do to deepen your relationship with Susie? Go back to your section and look over the items on deepening your relationship with Nurturers now.

Chamber	*Name*	*Style*	*To Do*
1.	Susie	Nurture	Send her a card acknowledging how important she is, schedule lunch with just her, ask her how I can help her.
2. ... etc.			

Now it's your turn.

BNI – *Name*	*Style*	*To Do*
1.		
2.		
3.		
4.		
5.		

Chamber – *Name*	*Style*	*To Do*
1.		
2.		
3.		
4.		
5.		

Rotary – *Name*	*Style*	*To Do*
1.		
2.		
3.		
4.		
5.		

Prof. Assn. – *Name*	*Style*	*To Do*
1.		
2.		
3.		
4.		
5.		

School – *Name*	*Style*	*To Do*
1.		
2.		
3.		
4.		
5.		

Church – *Name*	*Style*	*To Do*
1.		
2.		
3.		
4.		
5.		

Other – Name	Style	To Do
1.		
2.		
3.		
4.		
5.		

You now have a very detailed list of the next steps that you can take in order to deepen your most treasured relationships. Some of you may be thinking this is a lot of work. You are correct. We stated early on that referral marketing is not an overnight process. Building relationships takes time, especially developing incredibly high-quality relationships – which is where we want to take you!

Our suggestion is to focus on your top four best relationships and complete your To Dos as soon as you possibly can. Deepening your best relationships first can bring you measurable results in a short amount of time. It also gives *you* the most enjoyment, too!

Whenever you feel like your relationships have become stagnant, or simply are not bringing you the type of results they used to, come back to this chapter and see how you can take the appropriate steps to improve your relationships.

> ***"Deepening your best relationships first can bring you measurable results in a short amount of time and just so happens to give you the most enjoyment too!"***

CHAPTER 9
What Motivates Each Behavioral Style?

Motivation: the biological, emotional, cognitive or social forces that activate and direct our behavior.

Put simply, it's the reason why you act the way you act.

Why did you get out of bed this morning? What made you wear those shoes today? What has you going 75 mph in a 55 mph zone? What makes you attracted to that particular business person? What makes you choose to go to that networking event? Why did you want to talk to that person and stay away from the other one?

Motivation can be very tricky to understand. Humans are incredibly complex on one hand but on the other hand so easy to figure out when you understand behavioral styles.

When you think of what motivates you, it can be a multitude of things. Some motivation is a temporary situation. Say you don't enjoy numbers or accounting, yet at the end of the month you want to receive your paycheck. You may be temporarily motivated to do the accounting necessary to generate the paycheck.

However, if you thought about a career in accounting, it would make you sick to your stomach. Many people make an incredible living in this profession, so obviously you wouldn't die if you had to do that forever. But you are definitely not motivated to work with numbers on a regular basis.

The motivation that we would like to discuss now is the "how you are wired" variety. It's a motivation that may have been with you forever.

If you're a parent, have you ever noticed that your children are "wired" differently? Did you notice what motivated them before they could even speak? Did they want independence or to hold their own things? At times did they seem to not need you?

Or maybe your child had a knack for taking stuff apart and putting it back together, had to have 12 toys to play with to be happy or maybe they simply wanted time with you. Can you see how this is related to the four behavioral styles?

The independent baby could be the Go-Getter. The baby who is taking everything apart and putting it back together could be the Examiner. The baby who has to have 12 toys to play with or they get bored could be the Promoter. The baby who just wants time with you to feel safe could be the Nurturer.

Now, we want to remind you of the fact that you are a blend of all four styles, so we understand the above example isn't clear cut. We just want you to start thinking in this format. It will allow you to see people in a different way.

Now, how about some stories about us?

Ivan the Childhood Entrepreneur

When I was 11 years old, I missed the bus to school one day. The school was only two miles way, and I had time, so I started walking.

Along the way I passed a gas station that had a small store attached to it. My eye caught some beautiful lollipops – big, red strawberry-flavored suckers. They only cost a nickel (I'm probably aging myself with that information!) so I bought four or five of them and headed on to school. A friend saw what I had and asked if he could buy one. I said sure – for a dime. He bought it right away! That day I sold all the lollipops but the one I kept for myself… and I saw a great business opportunity.

The next day I walked to school again, this time buying a dozen lollipops. I sold them all before school let out for the day. I did this the next day, and the next… for almost a month, very happy at my markup and the money that I was starting to see growing from my lollipop enterprise.

Then one day, I got called into the vice principal's office. He asked me if I were selling candy at school. I said yes, indeed, and started to share with him the exciting story of how I was doubling my money. Before I could get very far, he interrupted me to say that I was not allowed to sell candy at school, and that if I continued, I would be expelled!

I was shocked. In fact, I immediately thought of the many fundraisers I had already seen at school by that time, which sold – you guessed it – candy. I asked the vice principal why it was okay for candy to be sold at school for fundraisers but I couldn't do the same thing. His only answer was a cryptic, "It's different."

That was my first experience in business and even though a "government regulation" shut it down after only a month, it was obvious from that early time in my life that I was a Go-Getter.

Tony Takes Charge, Even at an Early Age

As a child Tony typically busied himself with things—puzzles, blocks, game shows, or sports—that keep him occupied for hours. He delighted in showing his mom and dad the fruits of his labors. He exhibited tell-tale traits early in life.

He seldom responded to stranger's overtures. In fact, his mother said, he usually ignored them or looked at them as though he was thinking, "Who is this person, and what does she want?" He seemed to focus on his own preferred results soon after infancy. By an early age, he demanded to be read to at bed time to the point where his parents contemplated burning his books in protest!

When Tony temporarily lost his parent in a public setting, his eyes began to brim with tears, but he usually held his feelings inside instead of crying as he actively searched for the missing parent. Once taught to do so, he quickly sought clerks, security guards or police if he wanted help locating his errant parent, other person or things that interested him.

Tony, also often tried to take charge of the situation, especially when he didn't get his way. For instance, he would hold his breath until he turned blue. Parents often describe children like little Tony as headstrong or difficult, but understanding the child's need for near-complete control over his environment can yield surprising benefits.

Allowing kids like Tony to have authority over pets, toys, their own rooms, or other personal activities can channel their natural need for control in a positive way. Otherwise, they may frustrate their siblings in an effort to parent them. Tony's siblings usually piped up, "Mom, he thinks he's the boss and he's not!"

Dawn the Competitor

As a baby my Mom tells me that I was very independent, always on the go, very active and extremely curious. She also recalls me taking a few too many risks!

The interesting part is that when I was curious about something, I would look at it or touch it and then be done with it. My curiosity was over, so I had no need for it. I also had a knack for climbing up and down steps. Anytime there were steps around I would constantly go up and down, up and down. As a kid, I would stay outside all day long. It didn't matter if I was by myself or with my friend Susan; I was totally content either way.

One afternoon when Susan and I were hanging out by our pond catching tadpoles, and all I can remember is that I had to catch more than she did. I don't know why. We didn't have a bet or anything, but in my head I simply had to catch more. Other times, Susan and I would build separate forts and see whose was the best and then play in that fort for the rest of the day. Guess whose was typically the best? Yep, mine!

So, can you see how the "childhood stories" are completely relevant to who we are today? Motivation is motivation no matter what age you may be!

Motivation and Style

Let's discuss the motivation of each of the styles next. Remember, we are going to keep this focused on your referral marketing efforts. So, even though these strategies also apply to your personal life, most of the examples will be drawn from business. We want to stay true to our mission of showing you how your behavioral style is affecting your referability!

Go-Getters are motivated by –

- Being right
- Being in charge
- Looking good
- Winning
- Being the best
- Prestige
- Getting results

Nurturers are motivated by –

- Helping others
- Building quality relationships
- Involvement
- Making sure people feel comfortable
- Being appreciated
- Being of service

Promoters are motivated by –

- Having fun
- Freedom
- Meeting new people
- Recognition
- Connecting people
- Being famous

Examiners are motivated by –

- Processes
- Information
- Systems
- Knowledge
- Progress
- Perfectionism

Let's take a look at how these traits look and sound like in the business networking world.

We are going to give you random sets of phrases. Knowing how people are motivated, we would like you to write down which style you think would state each phrase.

NO... don't look ahead Go-Getters just to get all of the right answers. And Examiners, it really is okay if you are not perfect. Promoters... looking ahead would be easier, but we have made this super easy – you can do it! And Nurturers, won't it be nice when you can hear these phrases and understand how someone is motivated... do you think you could help them even more? Sure!

PHRASE	***STYLE***
"If everyone else is going, I'll go."	______________
"What does the agenda look like?"	______________
"Oh, it would be a pleasure to take care of that for you."	______________
"If it's the biggest event, then I have to be there!"	______________
"I'll be in charge of that."	______________
"Can we figure out some sort of structure to this?"	______________
"Ya know, I had a great time talking to you!"	______________
"The next step for us should be to understand the details of each of our businesses."	______________

PHRASE	***STYLE***
"I need to know more about your business to get you better referral results."	________________
"Hey, could we have lunch so we can hang out more and even chat about a little bit of business?"	________________
"I was hoping I could spend some more time with you at some point to really learn more about you and your business. Would that be okay with you?"	________________

Here is a trick question... be careful how you answer!

"How many people will be there?"	________________

We started with phrases that have some distinctive language in them to help you realize which style would be saying each phrase. But this last phrase is a trick question for good reason. The question itself is pretty straightforward. Someone could answer it directly with the correct answer. OR... you could find out the motivation behind the question by asking, "Well, why would you like to know?"

You could wind up with four different answers, such as:

1. "Well, I typically do better in smaller crowds as large crowds seem to be a waste of time for me. I like to meet just a few people and then leave." You may be talking to an Examiner.
2. "I was wondering if I could bring a few other people with me. There are a bunch of us who like to go to events together; it makes it a lot more fun!" Maybe you are speaking with a Promoter.
3. "If it's big enough I will probably come, but if not, it's not worth my time." Short and direct. You may be talking to a Go-Getter.

4. "Oh, I was just wondering if they might need any help and if I any of my friends are attending so I could spend some time with them, too." That's a Nurturer.

Do you see how you can ask a clarifying question to determine how someone is motivated? And this is just one simple example. Are you starting to see the differences in language between the four styles? It really is something to listen for as it gives you lots of clues into the person's behavioral style.

Now that you understand more about how the styles are motivated, we MUST put in a very clear warning. If you utilize this motivation section for the wrong intent, to hurt people or use them in any way shape or form, just know that it will come back to you. We have all seen this material used for the wrong reasons, and we promise you the people manipulating others have paid for it dearly.

When we understand how people are motivated we can –

- *Work with them more easily*
- *Be aware of situations that might come up while working with them*
- *Know how to explain projects or plans with ease*
- *Acknowledge when something has become stagnant and possibly re-motivate them in the proper way*

Wouldn't this be extremely helpful for you to know as you are deepening your referral relationships?

As you can see, understanding someone else's motivation can give you unique insights while developing a relationship. When you add in being able to speak the same language as that person... now you have some magic happening! In Chapter 10 we will show you how to work within each style's motivation while speaking each style's language. Yes, you are about to learn four new languages and anyone can do it!

Go-Getters: Are you ready? Examiners: Does that sound like the perfect next step? Nurturers: Do you feel like that would help you? Promoters: How cool will that be?

CHAPTER 10
Learning the Languages of All Four Behavioral Styles

Language is a very unique part of building relationships. When it comes to foreign languages, language can include or exclude someone. When you travel overseas and you do not speak the native language, it can be difficult to get your point across. If you know just a tiny bit of the foreign language and you are speaking with natives, you have to wait until they are done to have someone explain to you what just transpired.

It's the same experience when you are working with the different behavioral styles. You are including people in conversations when you speak their language, and you are excluding them when you do not. Okay, you might not be fully excluding them, but you could definitely be turning them off. Do you agree?

We hope you do, as we see it happening on a regular basis. If someone just took the time to speak the other person's language, the encounter between the two of them would have been so much better.

We have a very strong opinion that if you want to consider yourself an expert on behavioral styles, then you will want to master the four different languages of each style. Mastering the language of each style is comparable to a chef mastering the art of sauces. Can you imagine any renowned chef not knowing how to prepare gourmet sauces?

Well, we can't imagine anyone considering themselves an expert in behavioral styles without mastering the languages of each style. By the way, this is by no means as difficult as learning a foreign language. In fact, you will simply work on your word selection, pace and tonality. Sounds easy, right?

The toughest part of actually accomplishing this on a regular basis is to *choose* to speak another language. When we talk to people about actually speaking the other languages, we always have them consider their intention. Intention is a very powerful subject. If your intention is to manipulate people, then you will. However, if your intention is to have a more enjoyable experience and make others feel comfortable, then you can obviously make that happen, too. We want the latter example for you!

"As a Senior Director Consultant in the San Francisco Bay Area, the behavioral styles program has been immensely valuable. Working with a team of 50+ entrepreneurial volunteers and supporting 2300 business professionals, behavioral styles has been critical in meshing the team together and collaborating with and supporting all of the members.

"Even more important is the fact that I have a much greater awareness of a) what might be going on when I am not 'clicking' with someone and then being able to adapt to that and b) what I need to do when I have a relationship gone astray so that I can more quickly bring it back to a more conducive relationship.

"As a marketing trainer and coach I find I use this material each and every day in dealing with people!"

Trey McAlister • BNI SF Bay Senior Director Consultant • www.bnisfbay.com

Can you imagine how much more referable you can become if you could speak the four different languages? The possibilities are endless. In Chapter 12, we will be discussing the importance of a diversified network. And yes, one of the diversifications will be by behavioral styles. Therefore, being comfortable, knowledgeable, fluent and excited about using these four different languages will bring dramatic changes to your network.

Just a quick question: Did you see how the last sentence was written? Can you recognize the four different words that appeal to the four different styles?

Comfortable = *Nurturer*
Knowledgeable = *Examiner*
Fluent = *Go-Getter (it makes them look good)*
Excited = *Promoter*

We have used this verbiage throughout the book, so keep looking for it as we go along! It is amazing to see how easy it is to write and speak like this once you are fluent in the languages!

One last thing before we begin giving you some specific words and phrases to use with the four different behavioral styles. In Chapter 14, we will be elaborating on how to adapt to the other styles without being or feeling "fake." This is definitely a concern for the Nurturers. We understand and, again, this is where your intention comes into play.

It's not "being fake" when you use a selection of words that makes others feel more comfortable with you – you're honoring them!

What if just by knowing someone's style you could immediately have them engage in a better experience with you? One of the main questions we receive is: "How do I speak their language when it sounds so foreign to me when it comes out of my mouth?"

Don't all languages seem really foreign until you become more fluent in them? If you were to go to Spain right now, and you can speak Spanish, would you? Yes, of course! If you are not fluent, wouldn't you feel a little awkward?

Why do we speak their language when we are fluent in it? It's easier for the native people, plain and simple. It's not "being fake" when you use a selection of words that makes others feel more comfortable with you – you're honoring them!

The Language of Each Behavioral Style

Below you will find a list from A-Z of single words or phrases that will definitely appeal to each one of the styles. When speaking with the different styles, be sure to add these words and phrases into your conversation.

Go-Getters

Accomplish, Achieve, Assertive, Bold, Bottom-line, Compete, Confidence, Delegate, Done, Enterprising, Firm, Goal-oriented,

Get it done, Gutsy, Hustle, Independent, Jet set, Know-how, Lead, Leader, Manage, Make it happen, No-nonsense, Opportunity, Powerful, Productive, Qualified, Quality, Results, Strong, Take charge, THE best, Top, Ultimate, Upgrade, Valuable, What's next, Win, Xclusive, Yes - I got it, Zeal

Promoters

Adventure, Awesome, Bling, Chat, Creative, Delicious, Dude, Easy, Enthusiastic, Energy, Epic, Fabulous, Fun, Fun loving, Great, Hope, Incredible, Inspirational, Joke, Knack, Love, Motivational, New, OMG (oh my gosh), Optimistic, Popular, Quick, Really?, Simple, Sooooo cool, Soooo ready, Sooooo [just about any word here], Talk, Temptations, Terrific, Unique, Vision, Wish, Xceptional, Yes! (typically with a high five), Zest for life!

Nurturers

Approachable, Authentic, Believable, Balance, Calm, Comfortable, Dependable, Down to Earth, Enjoyable, Fair, Genuine, Giving, Grateful, Gracious, Help, Helpful, Insight, Joyful, Kind, Kindhearted, Loyalty, Meaningful, Natural, Nice, Open, Patient, Peace, Peaceful, Proper thing to do, Quiet, Relational, Reach out, Share, Steady, Thoughtful, Togetherness, Truly, Understand, Useful, Unity, Value, Warm, Xtra care, Yes - I'd love to help, Zen

Examiners

Analyze, Because, Calculation, Consistent, Deliberate, Detail, Effective, Efficient, Facts, Frugal, Gradual, Historical data, Information, Judge, Knowledge, Lineup, Measure, Make sense?, Necessary, Order, Practical, Predictable, Perfection, Question, Reserved, Schedule, Structure, Systems, Time, Thoroughness, Uphold the standards, Validate, Warranty, Watchful, Xpectation, Yes - I believe that is accurate, Zero

Are you going to be able to memorize all of these words, keep them in the forefront of your mind and use all of them in each and every conversation that you have with each style? Probably not. So just pick a few that appeal to you and use them often. Just like speaking a foreign language, it gets easier the more you practice it!

How Dawn Speaks to Each Style

When speaking to a large group of people, I always make sure to include each style's language throughout my presentation, especially at the beginning, to engage them all. My four favorite words are results, fun, help and effective.

My opening used to be as simple as this: "If I can help you get more results, be more effective, help other people and have some more fun in your life, would today's presentation be worth it for you?" Another example would be: "My objective with you today is to share with you some specific referral marketing knowledge that will be simple, fun and easy to implement. I will provide you with a way to help others in your network and ensure that you will create the best referral results ever!"

Can you see how I incorporated all four styles in each example? Once you practice it for oh, 20 years or so, it does become natural *I promise!* Today, I don't really have to even think about it; it's the unconscious competence stage. A quick tip for you: Does your website include language for all four styles? Something to think about!

A quick tip for you:

Does your website and brochures include language for all four styles?

Now that we know some of the right words to use with each style, what about “bad words”? Yes, there are bad words, too! Here is a short list of some of the worst things you can say to each style.

Go-Getter

Go-Getters hate anything that makes them look bad, especially in front of others, like...

- You’re wrong
- I bet you can’t
- You’re not good enough to do X
- You can’t handle that
- You’ll never get that done

Promoter

Promoters run away from all things negative, such as:

- It’s a lousy day
- Traffic stunk
- I hate the weather
- Business is really bad
- I hate my work
- You can’t come
- You weren’t invited
- You’re not wanted

Nurturer

Nurturers strongly dislike change, confrontation and seeing people reprimanded, verbally abused or simply being yelled at. For example…

- We have to change this now!
- We are going to talk about this now!

- We don't need your help
- We don't need you
- You're too sensitive

Examiners

Examiners get very frustrated with criticism and too many emotional situations, especially around business decisions.

- This isn't done right
- You made a mistake
- This work is below average
- You have to listen to how I feel

A Quick Exercise for Using Motivating Words

Obviously we want you to focus on the positive aspect and treat people the way they want to be treated. So let's do a quick exercise. Below, write down two names of people who are in your business network under each behavioral style. Then write down the next time you will be seeing them, the date will be fine. Next, what is an initial sentence or two that you could say to them at that meeting that would be 100% all about them and what they love to hear?

Name	***Style***	***Date***	***Sentence description***
___________	Go-Getter	___________	___________________________
			___________________________
			___________________________
___________	Go-Getter	___________	___________________________
			___________________________
			___________________________

Name	***Style***	***Date***	***Sentence description***
________	Promoter	________	________________
			________________
			________________
________	Promoter	________	________________
			________________
			________________
________	Nurturer	________	________________
			________________
			________________
________	Nurturer	________	________________
			________________
			________________
________	Examiner	________	________________
			________________
			________________
________	Examiner	________	________________
			________________
			________________

Remember, if they are a different style than you, then the words may seem a bit foreign. But again, the words are for them, not you. They will enjoy the words. You just have to make the choice to want to make them feel great!

A Story from Dawn: Role Playing

I was in England giving the Room Full of Referrals® Program to about 65 people. There was this one Go-Getter, let's call him Mark. I was sharing with the room that it is okay to speak in a much more casual way to the Promoters. In a live role-play I brought a Promoter up in front of the audience, let's call him Paul, and did an example of a conversation that might be had while networking. It went something like this:

"Hey there, I'm Dawn, how ya doing?"

Paul says, "I'm doin' just great, I'm Paul."

"Well, it's great to meet you Paul, what do you do?"

"I'm a photographer, and I absolutely love it!"

"Wow, I can hear it in your voice. What do you love about it, Paul?"

"I love the people, the events like weddings and babies I get to take pictures of, and I especially love seeing people so happy!"

"Oh my gosh, I never thought about it like that. Dude, you must wake up every day just excited and thrilled to work with all of your wonderfully happy clients!"

"Yep, I sure do! I have the best job in the world!"

Remember Mark the Go-Getter? At the end of the role-play, I glanced around the room and could see the absolute disgust on his face. He stood up and said, "There is no way I could or would ever say 'Oh my gosh' or 'dude' to someone; it's ridiculous!"

Now, remember I am a Go-Getter, and Mark was basically saying, "You did that wrong." So, knowing behavioral styles, I have a choice. I can argue with him directly in front of the room and make him look bad in front of everyone, or I can get the rest of the Promoters to tell him how it sounded to them. I choose the latter.

As the presenter it is never good to argue with your audience, especially the Go-Getters! I asked the Promoter group to raise their hand if they were 100% okay with the dialogue that happened in that conversation. Everyone raised their hand. Then I asked them to keep their hand up if they thought I was cool and would like to continue talking to me. You guessed it; everyone kept their hand up.

Mark quietly sat down and I told him, "Mark, I get it, and you're right... I get that it sounds weird and awkward to you, but the words are for them! Can you see how IF you choose to speak to them like that you build relationships faster and easier with better results? Is it possible that many of us Go-Getters have left money on the table because we have turned people off with our language? Would any of you Go-Getters like to get some of that back?!"

The whole group of Go-Getters raised their hand, including Mark!

Something to notice, why did I have "you're right" above in bold print? It can immediately put the Go-Getters at ease when you declare they are right. If I were to have said, "You're wrong, they like that language" and moved on, he would not have listened to another word I said.

We have covered the good words and the bad words for you. Now, it is simply your choice as to whether or not you will take the time to select the right language for the right person to impact their life in a positive way

"As a business consultant, speaking in a language that my clients can 'hear' is critical to the success of the relationship. Dawn's ability to explain the various ways that different behavioral styles can 'receive' information has been very helpful... and has allowed for more successful communication."
Shawn Jackson ESQ. • Business Development Attorney
Rohnert Park, California

CHAPTER 11
Gaining an Appointment with People of Each Behavioral Style

Now we'd like to show you a structured way to gain appointments with people you meet at networking events. This method will *save you time*, make them *feel wonderful*, get you *better results*, and it'll be *super easy* for you.

You can only go so far with a relationship at a networking event, especially if you are meeting a person for the first time. Therefore, part of the key to being a great networker is knowing how to gain appointments with specific people to further the relationship. If you try to meet up with everyone you met, you could waste a lot of time.

You can make a great impression with a new relationship when you ask for the appointment based on their behavioral style. Everything is very comfortable and easy for them, so they tend to say yes. Gaining the appointment by style is a definite skill as each style likes different approaches and vocabulary. Intention also plays a big part in this section. You have to be truthful, give clear expectations, set boundaries and, of course, be polite.

Our suggestion while networking is to always "give first." When you give first you are making an offer to help in some way. All styles need some sort of help, even if they are not willing to admit it right away (we're talking to you, Go-Getters!).

Here's how this section will proceed. The scenario is that you are at a networking function. You will meet each one of the styles, have a great conversation with them and believe that the two of you could help each other in your referral marketing efforts. You genuinely like each other.

Here is where we'll share with you how to ask for the appointment to take the next step in the relationship. It's kind of like asking for a date in the business world. Do it right, and you are excited about the meeting. Do it wrong, and you get rejected. If you have ever been rejected in the past, this chapter will be able to help you!

There is one BIG piece of the puzzle we haven't spoken about yet. We don't know of a networking function where everyone walks around with a name tag that has, say, "I am a Nurturer please treat me properly" on it. (Except for the Room Full of Referrals® program with Referral Institute. And no our name tags don't say that exactly. But everyone in attendance can see what style the rest of the attendees are, so at breaks they are able to mingle knowing this information!) So, let's quickly recap the tools we've already given you to begin to identify the four different behavioral styles while networking.

Behavioral Style Identification Tools:

- Understanding fast-paced/slower-paced and people-oriented/task-oriented
- The top 13 list of things to look for on page 12.
- The list of traits of each style page 52.
- The strengths and challenges list on pages 73.
- The good words lists on page 111.

You truly are equipped with the tools necessary to begin identifying other people's style. Just give it a shot! You may be guessing at first, but it will get easier.

Let's start with...

Go-Getters

- Be direct.
- Ask for only a short amount of time to start – say 30 minutes.
- Say you will come to them – makes it more convenient for them.
- Remind them of what you think you MIGHT be able to do for them but don't commit to it without knowing more about them.

- You may be able to agree on a date on the spot – do so!
- State that you will confirm everything via email or text (whichever they prefer) and send them a reminder email one day before – do not call them.
- Make sure to do what you say!
- Enjoy your really productive meeting!

Promoters

- Keep your energy up and smile.
- Let them know you are having a great time with them.
- Describe a bit about how you think you can connect them to other people who could be very interesting to them.
- Say something about a new hot spot that just opened or a cool place to meet. See if they could fit you into their busy schedule – makes them feel important.
- If they have their calendar available, select a date to meet for about an hour – you will need it as you may not get down to business quickly.
- Let them know you will call them to reconfirm everything.
- End by saying something about the possibilities from the two of you working together – describe the vision and have them buy into it!

Nurturers

- Make sure to really have them talk, and you listen!
- Share with them how you think the two of you would be really compatible, but you need to understand more about who they are and how they work with their clients.
- Tell them you would love to spend more time with them and see what could develop over the long-term.

- Do an option close[6] on the appointment and ask, "Would it be possible to look at our schedule and see if we might have some time to spend together in the next week or so OR would you like me to call you next week and go from there?" They tend to make a quicker decision when you do an option close.
- Whichever selection they make be sure to follow up.
- Ask if it would be okay if the location was a bit quiet so you could really be present with each other.
- Book out 1.5 hours just to be safe.
- Make it clear that you really want to get to know who they are in business because you truly think you can help them.
- Ask if it is okay to call them to confirm the appointment.
- Call to confirm and spend several minutes on the phone with them at that time.

Examiners

- Remember, you will need to ask them lots of questions as they may not give information out freely.
- Ask them if they are looking for ways to be more effective in their networking.
- Talk to them about *why* the two of you could be effective together.
- Ask if it would make sense for the two of you to spend more time together to figure out the details of how you could work together.
- Ask if a meeting at their office would be appropriate – makes it more convenient for them, and they don't waste time traveling somewhere.

[6] An option close is when you give someone two options that you are okay with, so whichever one they choose you are already fine with and can move forward.

- Do an option close on the appointment and ask, "Would it make sense to book an appointment now or would you like me to email you?" Again, they usually make a quick decision when you do an option close.
- Based on the answer complete that task.
- See if an email or text is the preferable way for you to confirm the appointment.
- Show up early to the appointment and be fully prepared with an agenda and lots of questions for them.

It's as easy as that! Can you see the amount of steps you will want to take with the Nurturers and Examiners? This is mainly due to their pace. They'll want to move a bit slower. Yet, when approached correctly, you can easily get them moving forward in the relationship. It all depends if you are treating them the way that they want to be treated or not!

You have just received a very simple, step-by-step formula for gaining more appointments with the people that you truly want to get to know better and build stronger relationships with.

One of your goals at a networking function could be to meet several new people. Once you meet them, you then must decide if you would like to continue the relationship. If you do it by behavioral style, we are positive you will gain better results, faster quality relationships, enjoy your networking more often and obviously make it a great experience for the other person to go through because *they* get treated appropriately!

CHAPTER 12
Developing a Diverse Network

As entrepreneurs, we realize you have choices in your business, and one of those choices is who you spend your time with. The people that you are networking with can have a positive effect on your business, a neutral effect or a negative effect.

Understanding how to intentionally develop a strong personal network will allow you to create the network you absolutely desire. Yet, were any of you trained how to develop your network? Did you take any classes on it in business school?

See, many of the business owners we work with share that they have basically fallen into a network versus created their own unique network. Some people got lucky and the network has been successful for them, others, well, not so much. The real question is: "How much time have you spent intentionally developing the perfect, diverse network for you?

Let's begin by having Ivan share with you his personal opinion about diversity and networking. Then we will come back and add in how behavioral styles can also play a huge role in the overall success of your network, especially your referral network!

Diversity and Networking
By Ivan Misner

When it comes to business networking, you never know who people know. One of the keys to being successful at building a powerful personal network is diversity.

In running a large business networking organization for the last two decades, I often speak to people who tell me they want to network exclusively with other business professionals who work with clients in a similar socio-economic target market. In other words – network with business professionals with similar clients. And even though they may not consciously have realized it, they were also seeking to work with those who had their same behavioral style(s)! Although it is good to include these people in your personal network, any attempt to network with that one style exclusively would be a tremendous mistake.

It's human nature to congregate with people who are very much like us. People tend to cluster together based on education, age, race, professional status, etc. The bottom line is that we tend to hang out with people who have similar experiences or perspectives as ours. Most of our friends and associates are often friends and associates with each other as well. The problem with this is that when we surround ourselves with people who have similar contacts, it may be difficult to make connections with new people or companies with whom we desire to do business.

A diverse personal network enables you to increase the possibility of including connectors or "linchpins" in your network. Linchpins are people who in some way cross over between two or more clusters or groups of individuals. In effect, they have overlapping interests or contacts that allow them to link groups of people together easily.

The best way to increase the number of linchpins in your network is to develop a diverse network – not a homogeneous one.

When it comes to networking, diversity is key because it allows us to locate these connectors. Connectors are the gateways to other people. They create shortcuts across groups and possibly even behavioral styles.

The best way to increase the number of linchpins in your network is to develop a diverse network – not a homogeneous one.

Having developed over 5,700 networking groups in more than 44 countries, I can categorically state that the strongest networking groups I've seen are generally ones that are diverse in many, many ways. And they include people from each behavioral style. The more diverse the network, the more likely it will include overlapping connectors that link people together in ways they would have never imagined.

I believe that one of the problems in understanding this concept is a somewhat built-in bias that many people have about networking with individuals that are outside their normal frame of reference. A good friend of mine in Boston, Patti Salvucci, once told me an amazing story that illustrates this point perfectly.

Patti runs dozens of networking groups for BNI in the Boston area. She was visiting one of the groups recently that met in a private meeting room at Fenway Park. She arrived a little early to the meeting and noticed an older gentleman setting up coffee mugs in preparation for the meeting.

Anyone who knows Patti knows that she is a master networker. True to form, she struck up a conversation with the man while waiting for members to arrive. In talking to him, she was really taken by the amazing sound of his voice. She mentioned to him that he had an incredible speaking voice and asked what he did before this. He informed her that he used to be a commentator for CNN!

He went on to tell her that in his later years, he wanted to work in a less hectic job and also live closer to his daughter. He decided to take on the job of managing the owner's suite at Fenway Park in Boston because it gave him an opportunity to be close to his family while having a less hectic career later in life.

Patti asked him about some of the people that he met during his time in broadcasting. He shared many great stories with her, including an interview with JFK a week before he was assassinated. He also talked about meeting Martin Luther King Jr. and Nelson Mandela. It was an interesting conversation that she genuinely enjoyed.

Later, when the meeting was in full swing, one of the regular members, Don, mentioned that he would really like to do a radio talk show someday and was looking for some contacts that could help him pursue this dream.

After the meeting, Patti asked Don, "Do you see that guy over there [pointing to the ex-CNN commentator]? Have you seen him before?" "Yeah," said Don, "He's the guy who sets up the coffee for our meeting." Patti said to Don, "Did you know that he used to be a broadcaster for CNN?" Don said, "Oh my God; I had no idea!!!"

Patti suggested that Don introduce himself and learn a little about the man he's seen every week for the last several months, because he may very well be able to make a connection for him in the broadcasting industry.

The lesson in this story is that he had seen the man on many occasions but had not struck up a conversation with him because he felt that they had little, if anything, in common. The truth is, when it comes to networking, not having a lot in common with someone may mean that they can be a connector for you to a whole world of people that you might not otherwise be able to meet.

The more linkages you can make between clusters of people, the stronger your network can be!

Some of the strongest networking groups I've seen over the last two decades are ones that are diverse in many ways. They have a good mix of members based not only on the usual aspects of race and gender, profession, age, education and experience – but also a solid representation from each of the four behavioral styles.

The more diverse your network, the more likely you are to make overlapping linkages between clusters of people. The more linkages you can make between clusters of people, the stronger your network can be.

If you wish to build a powerful personal network – branch out. Build a diverse network of professional contacts that include people that don't look like you, sound like you, speak like you, or have your background, education, or history. The only thing that they should have in common with you and the other people in your network is that they should be really good at what they do. Create a personal network like that, and you'll have a network that can help you succeed at anything.

Thanks, Ivan! Understanding that a diverse network is crucial is very important to your business. The deeper level to this concept is to now take action on creating your diverse network and add behavioral styles to the mix.

Remember, you have choices. Declare now that you will take a stronger stance in finding the *right* people to be in your network and that you will also develop the diversity by style too. Here's why - the different styles *give* referrals differently! That's right. Each style gives referrals just a little differently than the others, and it will affect *your* business revenue. Knowing this part of the equation can become vital in realizing a consistent flow of referrals.

We bet you'd like to know how it is that each of the styles give referrals differently, so let's start with the Promoters! Sorry Go-Getters, Promoters love to be in the spotlight, so we are going to start with them this time!

Promoters:

Imagine meeting a Promoter, and you hit it off! No matter what your style is (maybe you are an Examiner, and you adapted your style a bit etc.) you met and really enjoyed each other's company and have decided to go out to lunch to get to know each other better.

After just an hour of chatting about your businesses the Promoter says, "Ya know, Suzi really needs to talk to you. She is always complaining about X and I think you are great and she is going to love you. I'm gonna have her call you!" That week Suzi does call and the referral ends up as closed business for you.

You think wow, that was a pretty simple referral. I think this is going to be a great referral relationship.

What we would like to share with you is a few examples of tendencies that each style has around how they build relationships.

Plus, we'll go over when and how you can expect referrals to be given to you.

Promoters tend to:

- Give referrals quickly in a new relationship – as long as they LIKE you!
- Give a couple of referrals back-to-back – the new relationship is exciting to them and you are top of mind.
- Give referrals of people they have a lot of influence over – meaning they "tell" them they have to call you, and generally they do.
- Once the relationship is built, become sporadic in their referral giving – they have hot and cold streaks.

Ways Promoters could improve their giving:

- Keep your referral sources more top of mind so your consistency goes up.
- Be willing to qualify the prospect more thoroughly versus always using your influence.

Nurturers tend to:

- Spend time building the personal side of the relationship, before they ever give referrals.
- Not be interested in "pushing the referral." They are more concerned about the prospect and that everything is just right before referring them, sometimes to a fault.
- Only give the referral if they have a very strong relationship with the prospect.
- Give referrals that typically close – due to the fact that it is the right decision for both parties.

Ways Nurturers could improve their giving:

- Believe that people value your opinion.

- Be more open to starting a conversation on a referral sources behalf, especially when you know your friend needs the service.
- Understand that you are helping people to solve problems in their life – you are not trying to sell them on buying someone's service. It's a slightly different mindset and can really help you to see the reward your friend receives when you offer them a solution to their problems.

Examiners tend to:

- Need a lot time to gather information on your business, your expertise and you.
- Validate that you are a person of integrity before ever giving you a referral.
- Be reluctant to start conversations on your behalf.

Ways Examiners can improve on their giving:

- Be willing to have more one-to-one meetings with referral sources in the beginning of the relationship to speed up the time frame you need to gather information.
- Set up a process in your business to ask clients questions to see if they need other services that you could then refer out.

Go-Getters tend to:

- Give referrals quickly IF they think you are an expert and will make them look good.
- Like to give business to people who are already successful.
- Give both low-quality and high-quality referrals – low-quality if they aren't concerned about how you feel about them and high-quality if they want to impress you.

Ways Go-Getters can improve on their giving:

- Ask the prospect more qualifying questions so the referral isn't pushed on them.
- Set goals for how many referrals you would like to give to each of your best referral sources and then hit the goal.

When you take a look at what you have just learned here it is important to understand with whom you are spending your networking time.

If you are spending a lot of time with a Go-Getter at the beginning of the relationship – they may not need it. Show them you are an expert, make them look good, and you're all set. However, if you take that same approach with a Nurturer, they may find you hard to get to know, non-relational and all business, thus making them feel unimportant.

Imagine identifying four new people you would like to incorporate into your network because remember you are going to do this intentionally! Let's also assume that they are each one of the styles. Your expectation may be that they should all be referring you the same amount in the same initial time frame.

What really happens is the Promoter gives you a referral or two right away, and then nothing for months. Go-Getter gives you one, but it doesn't go so hot, then they don't give you any more. After two months of building the relationship, the Nurturer has mentioned to you that they are working on a possible referral for you. The Examiner after three to four months is willing to still meet with you but hasn't really mentioned any referrals just yet.

Can you see how bringing behavioral styles into the mix can truly help you to identify how and when people will begin to refer you? Have your expectations been off in the past?

A Story from Dawn: Two Clients Choose Different Strategies

I was recently working with a client who was adamant about never having an Examiner as a referral source. They were simply unwilling to take the time necessary to develop the relationship.

In the same time frame another client told me they were very nervous about bringing an Examiner on board as a referral source and at the same time very excited about it. They invested the necessary time into the relationship and even took some Referral Institute training together. This took a few months.

My client told me on our last coaching call that the Examiner has been their number one referral source for the past two months, and they are afraid they are not going to be able to keep up with Examiner! What was the difference in my two clients? The conscious choice they made.

Knowing your referral sources behavioral style will help you to understand the amount, the frequency and the longevity of the referrals you will receive from them.

See, each style has strengths and weaknesses in giving referrals and building relationships. When you intentionally create your referral network and are bringing new referral sources into your network, definitely identify which style they are so you can set the appropriate expectations of when they might start to refer you.

Now, there are exceptions to the above tendencies. This is not set in stone. We are always fascinated when people have certain expectations of other people, and they do not take into consideration the person's behavioral style and what they need to feel comfortable in the referral process!

Knowing your referral sources behavioral style will help you to understand the amount, the frequency and the longevity of the referrals you will receive from them. That's why you want to diversify your network by behavioral styles too!

CHAPTER 13
Training Your Referral Network by Behavioral Style

After years of seeing thousands of business owners get frustrated with the amount of referrals they receive, it has been very interesting to ask, "How are you training your network to bring you the referral business?"

Blank stares, looks of sheer confusion, eyebrows and shoulders up and "I don't know" is the reply most of the time.

It's a major dilemma in the business world. Businesses are looking for more referrals, the only place it comes from is other people. But the business owner takes no active part in actually training their network to bring them that referral business. Our guess is that the business owners feel it should come to them automatically. They believe people should already know instinctively who they want referred to them, how they should refer them, when they should refer them, why they should refer them and how often they should refer them.

Wow, doesn't that seem a tad bit overwhelming for a referral source to *just know*? Wouldn't it be nice if we took some responsibility for the amount of referrals or lack of referrals for our business? One of the philosophies of the Referral Institute, albeit a bit direct, is "It's all my fault."

Wherever your business stands currently is a direct result of the work and effort you have put into it. The same is true for your referral marketing efforts. Whether you're experiencing a lot of success with referrals, or you're dealing with little to no success with referrals, you will want to realize at some point that "It's all my fault." For our Nurturers, we sometimes say, "It's all our responsibility."

We encourage you to own your situation and then look forward to see how you can solve the issue. Be okay with wherever you are in your business at the moment and know it can be better. In fact, it can give you a spectacular life if you're willing to put in the time and effort it takes to develop it to that level.

The Referral Institute's Mission

By providing relevant referral marketing instruction, continuous support and compassionate consulting to develop a unified personal network, The Referral Institute creates communities of like-minded, successful entrepreneurs who generate amazing business and aspire to a spectacular life!

We feel that is a pretty powerful statement and are obviously enjoying the thousands of business owners from around the world that we are working with to create just that, a spectacular life... whatever that may be for them.

If you were going to pay attention to any chapter in this book, this is the one. There is an undeniable correlation between how many people in your network are thoroughly trained and the amount of referrals you receive. We are going to cover some more Referral Institute material here mainly because we are the world's leader on referral marketing.

Let's take a look at the three core competencies in referral marketing:

1. Gain the right referral marketing education.
2. Stay immersed in the information.
3. Get your referral network trained by the experts.

For the first core competency, we recommend that you check www.referralinstitute.com and look under Regional Headquarters to see if there is a local Referral Institute franchise in your area. That is the easiest way to gain the right referral marketing knowledge. They will offer a listing of the different programs they offer in their area. If you love to learn new things through training seminars or classes, this could be a great option for you. Plus, you would get connected with all of the other clients in your area as well.

We have also given you some books to think about throughout this book such as *The World's Best Known Marketing Secret, Building Business by Referral* written by Ivan and Mike Macedonio. Another book from Ivan and Mike is *Truth or Delusion, Busting Networking's Biggest Myths*. These two books will give you a great deal of information that you can definitely apply to your business immediately. If you prefer to learn through books and reading, this option may be the best for you.

There is also one-to-one consulting available to anyone in the entire world thanks to technology. For more information, please contact info@referralinstitute.com for a private session to direct you to the right referral marketing consultant for you. If you learn best from direct teaching and prefer to work exclusively one-to-one with an expert to create more accountability and success, this is the way to go.

Are you seeing what we are doing yet? If not, keep reading.

Core competency number two is all about staying immersed in the information. Did you know that it takes more than 10,000 hours to be a master at a given subject? It's true, 10,000 hours.

Immersion helps you understand, digest and have a deep appreciation for information. The main reason to stay immersed in information is so it becomes a habit to you. Once it's a habit you begin to fall into the category of unconscious competence. Referral marketing skills, techniques and tactics are pretty foreign to most business owners, so immersion is vital to creating those habits in your business.

You may want to get started sooner rather than later to ensure the optimal amount of success in your business!

Let's focus on the third core competency: getting your network trained by the experts. This is without a doubt the most frustrating part of your referral marketing efforts as the first two core competencies are all about you, which you have some control over. However, the third core competency is 100% about your ability to motivate people to get the proper training.

What you may not realize is that they have to get trained in not just one but two different aspects of referral marketing. They must of course be firmly trained in who you are, why you do what you do and how you help people in your business. They must also be trained in core competency number one: the right referral marketing education.

If they know a lot about you, but know nothing about the strategies and techniques to making referrals easy, then they will have a difficult time referring to you. Vice versa if they have tons of referral marketing education but are not decisively trained on you and your business. They simply won't be inspired to help you.

Training on both you and Referral Marketing is an absolute must if you want to receive the absolute best results and have more fun with your relationships than you have ever had.

Training Your Network

Our focus here is to show you how to train your network by behavioral style. The "what" of training your network is a different book, class or consulting situation[7].

Many business owners miss a huge opportunity to treat people the way that they want to be treated when they begin training someone. They typically have only one way to train someone, either by reading a manual/website/brochures, watching a video, just learning "on the spot," or… we could go on and on. The key is it that all of the styles have a specific way they would like to be trained. How do we know this?

Imagine this, you have been hired to drive an 18-wheeler semi across the country.

You have absolutely no experience except driving a regular car. How do you want your instructor to train you to drive this immense piece of machinery that could do horrible damage not only to you but others over the course of 3,000 miles?

[7] The Referrals For Life® program is your best option for gaining this information.

Before you read any further, please write down your answer now on how you would want the instructor to teach you how to drive this truck.

____

____

____

____

____

____

____

This is actually a live training piece that we have done all over the world, and it is one of the funniest things ever. Visualize a room of 100 business owners at a training seminar. They are divided up into the four different behavioral styles, and they have five minutes to compile a list of how they would like to be trained to drive the 18-wheeler.

Each of the groups begins discussing the situation, and, of course, the Promoters are always the loudest. They typically come to the front of the room or where the stage is! The Nurturers form a circle and sit down so everyone can be seen and heard. The Examiners find an out of the way corner to discuss the puzzle while sitting down. And the Go-Getters get up, form a group while standing. Everyone is chiming in, and they are done in one to two minutes!

When the five minutes are up, the Promoters are typically the last ones back to their seats, the Go-Getters are waiting (impatiently) for the instructor to start again, the Examiners are wanting more time as they do not have a thorough enough list compiled, and the

Nurturers are making sure that everyone got a chance to share their opinion and feel included in the decision.

What are the actual results of the exercise? Here are the most popular answers from around the world for each style. See how your answers align with these.

Go-Getters

How would the Go-Getters like to be trained on how to drive the 18-wheeler?

- Give us the keys.
- Where is it parked?
- Let us figure it out.
- If we can't, we will ask the instructor a question or two.
- But we doubt we will need him.

Truly, we are not lying. We cannot tell you how many times that exact list comes up with the Go-Getters. Other answers include:

- We want the best instructor.
- Who needs a manual?
- You have 10 minutes to tell us the basics.
- How much money are we going to make for driving this thing cross-country.

Are you asking Go-Getters to invest hours and hours with you? Are you annoying them by telling them what they should be doing for you? What if you gave them the keys to drive your referral truck, and they knew what to do... could you be receiving a lot of new referrals right now?

Promoters

For the Promoters, their answers sound like this:

- Just show us once, and we will be okay!
- Don't worry... we can figure it out.

- How fast can we go?
- Can our friends ride in the back?

Those are the top four answers for the Promoters. Here are some additional answers that come up regularly:

- Is the instructor cool and are they gonna hang out with us?
- We get to use the horn a lot right?
- Can we get a bright red truck with flames?
  (Comes up at least 60% of the time.)

Notice how it is all about people, fun and keeping it simple! It really is not about how to drive the truck, but what the experience of driving it is going to be like.

How would you describe the experience you give others as they are learning about you? Do you ask them to read your website or brochure? Maybe you have them experience your work once. Is that enough? What system do you have to ensure that you are providing a fun and easy learning atmosphere for the Promoters?

Nurturers

Here are the answers for the Nurturers:

- We want one–to-one time with the instructor.
- We want them to sit in the driver's seat and show us everything hands on.
- We want to understand all of the truck's safety features.
- We want the instructor to be a Nurturer too.
- We want to feel encouraged and confident.

Is this a little bit different than the other two styles? Here are some additional answers that came up regularly:

- We want to practice in a large empty parking lot for a few days before we get on the road.
- We especially want to know how to back up so we don't hit anything or anyone.

- We want the instructor to be kind and patient with us.
- We would like the instructor to travel with us for the first day.

Can you see a major shift in the pace of how all of this would come about? Pace is a very big differentiator between the styles! If you are simply asking Nurturers to refer you "because," it's just not enough for them. What will your process be to get them through all of the information they will need about you?

Examiners

Here are the answers for the Examiners:

- Before we receive training, we need to know what credentials the instructor has, how much it costs, what is our time investment and what is our return on that investment.

In many cases the Examiners never get to listing the answers for actually driving the truck because they are spending their time talking about all of the details that would need to happen before they are able to even drive it. For those that do get past it, here are a few more answers:

- We want to read the entire manual before we meet with the instructor.
- Videos would also be good before meeting the instructor.
- We would like a company that has a simulator so we can practice way before going on the road.
- Once we meet with the instructor, we would like to see the agenda of what will be required of us.
- We would like a thorough document about the route to take, where to make stops and all details about the 2,987 mile trip.

Just a little different? Can you see all of the analyzing up front? Before they can even get started, they have to understand many other components first. Remember, they need things to be accurate and thorough. How accurate and thorough are you in training your network? If you don't have any structure to your training yet, how successful will you be in training Examiners who can offer you a consistent source of referrals?

You might be wondering what this example has to do with training your network in how to refer you more often. Well, it depicts how they like to learn. Some learn fast, while others need more time. Some need basics, and they will figure the rest out later. Others need to know close to everything before they even get started – which, by the way, to them is just the starting point. Some need to know you care or want have fun with you, while others are simply looking for their return on investment.

These are all crucial for you to understand if you truly want to treat others the way that *they* want to be treated. We promise you will have a much higher success ratio in training your network if you take the learning styles into consideration.

Let's give you a list of how each style would like to be dealt with in the training arena.

Go-Getters

- Short time frames, they think fast and can often be a step ahead of you.
- Not too many details – just the basics.
- Start out with asking them, "What do you need to know about me?" They already know what they need from you.
- Make it convenient for them – maybe meet at their office.
- Let them go out and try to refer you and then have them check back as to how it went – they like to see results quickly.

Promoters

- Keep things light and simple – not too technical or intense.
- Teach them in a very visual way if possible.
- They learn by doing – so role playing is a great option.

- Make sure to have some fun on every appointment with them – remember it is about the experience.
- Keep them interested by using a reward if you two accomplish X – they will work hard for the prize.
- Give lots and lots of recognition when they do the right thing.
- Did we say have fun with them already? It really is the key to keeping them around long-term.

Nurturers

- Spend quality time with them answering any questions they may have.
- Move cautiously and don't ask for too much at the beginning.
- Provide them with an opportunity to experience your work if possible. This will give them the hands-on involvement that they like.
- Encourage them often and let them know verbally one–to-one when they have done something wonderful for you.
- Remind them that the relationship goes both ways and that you want to help them, too.
- Know that if the Nurturer does not trust you enough, it's very unlikely that they will ever generate referrals for you – develop trust first and foremost.
- Provide them a lot of training on qualifying a prospect for you. They tend to shy away from the "sales" part of referral marketing when they actually have to sell someone on you.

Examiners

- Discuss the possibilities of even having a referral relationship and what that might look like.
- Set some initial expectations of each other.

- Look at the amount of time investment the two of you would be willing to have.
- Then begin discussing what material, knowledge or information they would need to move forward.
- Create a process that each of you will commit to generate referrals regularly for each other.
- Have regularly scheduled meetings and track the success of the relationship.

We have to ask you, "Have you been teaching people about you and your business the same way to everyone?"

Of course, you always bring your style to the table first. Now you have an additional tool within your reach to ensure that people are enjoying working with you and learning how to refer you. Realizing this one piece of the puzzle about behavioral styles can really infuse life into your network. They will be much more motivated to work with you and learn from you when they feel better about the process and the outcome!

Who are four people that you commit to setting a meeting with about referring each other more often (with appropriate training)?

	Name	Style	How will I adapt to their style?
1.	____________	____________	____________
2.	____________	____________	____________
3.	____________	____________	____________
4.	____________	____________	____________

CHAPTER 14
The Tools to Help You Adapt

As stated in an earlier chapter, many of you will have concerns about coming across as fake if you begin to adapt to other styles. This chapter is dedicated to giving you the tools you need to make sure that is not the case.

Fake is defined as a person or thing that appears or is presented as being genuine but is not. So, the real question is: "Are you being genuine when you adapt?" If you are genuine, then you will not have any issues at all. We know it sounds simple, and yet maybe it isn't that simple.

We have spent decades learning, being aware, acknowledging and adapting to all this material. For us, it isn't about being fake. It's about honoring others. But it does require a few tools to be able to get to that point. Our objective is to help you speed up implementation of this material and have you take years off the learning curve, if you will.

The first and best tool that you have is your mind! Yes, your mindset around this information will help you tremendously in learning and adapting. Your mindset is a set of beliefs or a way of thinking that determines someone's behavior and or outlook. If your mindset is that you will just treat everyone the same, then that determines your behavior. And you will accomplish just that – treat everyone the same.

If your mindset is that you would like to honor other people's styles as you work with them, then that will affect your behavior AND get you better results, too!

Whether you have studied behavioral styles for years, have taken some sort of assessment or are reading this book and learning about behavioral styles for the first time ever, you have a mindset, or belief, about behavioral styles right now. We would like you to take just a moment and describe below what your current mindset is about behavioral styles.

You may be overwhelmed with the amount of information, you may think this is super easy, you may be reluctant to trying to use it or you may have been ready during Chapter 5 to start using it. Whatever your state of mind at the moment, that is where you are starting from. We can develop and grow from there, so please be as descriptive as possible!

My current mindset is:

____

____

____

____

Okay, you now know where you are starting from. Next, we would like you to write what you would like your mindset to be:

____

____

____

____

Did the phrase unconscious competence come up for you? Or maybe "to be aware and honor other people's styles"? No matter where you are or where you want to be, here are several tools that will help you get started on the pathway of adapting to other people's styles without being fake!

Let's go a bit deeper with the whole mindset scenario as there are several sub-headings under mindset that we would like to discuss. The first is awareness.

Awareness is described as having knowledge of something from observing it or having been told about it. So, guess what? We have been telling you about behavioral styles for the entire book, AND you have been observing people's behavioral styles for your entire life.

So, you are thoroughly aware that they exist and can help or hinder you in your relationships! Therefore, the truth of the matter is you are aware. The better question is, "Are you applying it to your daily activities with others?"

See, the three of us have heard for years, "Oh, yeah I know this information already" or "I heard this stuff years ago." But that doesn't mean they are using it in their daily lives. For some reason people tend to use behavioral styles only in certain situations.

If they learned about it at work, then they might apply it at work but not in their home life. Or if they learned about it through one job then leave, they don't apply it at the next job. It is very strange to us. People are all around you, at the office, at home, at the mall, on the golf course, at the charity event. Can't you use behavioral styles everywhere there are people? Absolutely!

If you are aware of behavioral styles and there are people around you, then you could be using this material! Here is what awareness might look like in real life.

A Story from Dawn: The Millionaire's Style

I was working with my mentor, let's call him Josh, and we had a 30-minute call scheduled. I called in right on time and began by asking how his wife was doing... how his four children were doing in school and in sports... and I even asked what they did over the weekend. Finally, 10 minutes in, I began talking about the purpose of the call. I wasn't really prepared, so my questions were all over the place and not really well-structured.

I got off the phone with this multi-millionaire feeling lousy. I felt like I wasted his time and, most importantly, I felt like we weren't really connecting. Then I said, "How could I have made this better for him, so he wants to keep mentoring me?" I started to think about his behavioral style and here is what our next call sounded like:

"Hi Josh, I have seven thoroughly prepared questions for you. It should take about 20 minutes. Does that work for you?"

He said, and I quote, "GO!"

Yikes, I thought, okay, question number one... he answered it. Question number two... he answered it. And so on. When I finished with the seventh question he asked if I had any other questions. I said no, and he replied, "Great call; I will talk to you next week!"

This went on for our next three calls, and then a funny thing happened. He actually called me on a random day and said, "I wanted to let you know that I have really been enjoying our mentor calls, and I was wondering if you have anything else you need help with." Wow, I thought, here is a multi-millionaire calling me and wanting to help me!!

For months after that he consistently called me during the week in addition to our normally scheduled calls. Years later I asked him what changed, and he said, "You were the only person I was mentoring who got it and treated me the way that I wanted to be treated. So it felt more comfortable working with you than all the others combined!"

What a win-win situation. He enjoyed the process more. I had an incredible mentor experience plus learned a ton from this man. All because I applied behavioral styles to our weekly phone calls and honored his style!

How does Dawn's story apply to awareness? Well, if you think about her story, she didn't go into the first call appropriately. But after the call ended she had a feeling that it didn't go very well. That is awareness. She became aware that something was *off* between the two of them. She then looked at behavioral styles to see if she could honor his style better. And the results… well, would you like a multi-millionaire calling you weekly to help you in your business?

How can you become more aware? Take a look at your calendar and go back to the past month or two. Look at the people you had appointments with and recollect how they went. Did you feel good about the appointments, were you unsure, did they go fabulously?

By examining an appointment afterwards, you can become aware. You can also become aware if a conversation is going okay right in the moment. It simply depends on your level of awareness and how quickly you can adapt.

"I've taken Room Full of Referrals™ many, many times over the past seven years. I felt it would help in my relationships with my clients. I WAS WRONG.

"It has helped me with my relationships with my clients/my family/my employees/my children… and most important with the Love of My Life. It has shown me how to interact with those I see/talk to/communicate with every day.

"The more often I take the class the better my communication skills are honed. You don't go to Toastmaster's once to learn how to present yourself. You DON'T go to Room Full of ReferralsTM once. Continued education is the key to success and Room Full of Referrals is the key to unlock success in your life."

Jay A. Zemansky • Sadler & Co. Inc. • Kentfield, CA
www.sadlerinc.com

Our best suggestion is to stay in tune with how the other person is responding to you or not. Ask clarifying questions and begin to figure out their behavioral style so you can speak their language and treat them the way that they want to be treated.

The next tool you have is intention. Intention is a very powerful thing. Intention is something you plan to do. It's your aim, your objective, your purpose. If your intention in life is to treat others with respect, honor and integrity, then fantastic! You are on the right track and behavioral styles will simply take your intention and develop it even further.

If your intention is to use this material to deceive, thwart or manipulate people, we are very sorry that we have armed you with this knowledge. However, we do believe 100% that if you do choose the latter path, you'll attract it to your own life, so just be warned!

A Story from Dawn: Jack the Go-Getter

I will never forget this! I was speaking on the East Coast (I am being vague on purpose), and I was told that there was an expert in the room who does DiSC® assessments for business owners. Throughout my presentation to about 150 people, I promoted "Jack" as someone the audience could talk to after the program if they wanted local help on the material from a DiSC® expert. I must have mentioned Jack's name at least 15 times in the presentation.

I began wrapping up, and once again mentioned that for more information or to take a DiSC® assessment locally, the audience should see Jack when, to my disbelief, Jack stood up in the audience waved to everyone and walked to the front of the room. He grabbed the microphone out of my hand and began to tell people that he could work with them... he had been doing this for 20 years (which was longer than I had been doing it)... he quoted his prices for a consultation... he told people to come see him afterwards... I could go on and on.

He must have spoken for three minutes, which is a long time when I never asked him to even get out of his seat. Did I mention he grabbed the microphone right out of my hand?!

Jack didn't sponsor the event. He didn't pay for any of the positive promotion that I gave him during the presentation.

I never said he would have any time to speak during the presentation. And I surely never asked him to interrupt my closing comments so that he could SELF-promote his business and try to hard close my audience on purchasing an assessment from him!

Guess what behavioral style Jack was... yep, a Go-Getter. But not just any Go-Getter, a Go-Getter with the wrong intentions. Instead of being humble, grateful for the promotion and the call to action of "go see Jack" that I had given him freely, he chose to "take the stage" and take over the show.

The most interesting part is that afterwards I had no less than 20 people come up to me and say, "I was going to get that DiSC® assessment, but I didn't like the way that guy talked to the audience, and he was selling really hard... do you know anyone else in the area that offers it?!"

WOW, think of all of the clients he lost in that moment. What were his intentions? We will never know for sure, but how many of you would have the guts to grab a microphone out of the hand of the official presenter in front of 150 other people?

Tools of Service

Another tool you may not have thought about is your level of service. Serving others is a privilege. When you believe in serving other people you have a true heart to help them, see the best in them and give to them freely.

It's so wonderful to see other people respond to you when you serve them in their behavioral style and put them first. Again, you may be the only person in the conversation that has this knowledge. So it's your responsibility to serve others with this knowledge and put them ahead of your needs.

"Whomever wants to become great; must become a servant." Mark 10:43

Here is another real life story from Dawn.

A Story from Dawn: The Gala Dinner

I was driving into San Francisco about 10 minutes from crossing the Golden Gate Bridge, when my now ex-husband calls and says, "Hey, I got tickets to that gala event tonight, so we are going!"

Looking at the jeans and sweater I had on, I say, "No, we're not. I have nothing to wear." He says, "I know. You have one hour to go to Macy's and get what you need, I will see you here in an hour!"

I start driving like a mad woman. I valet the car at Macy's and make a bee-line for the dress department. As I walk down the aisle I can see a young gal with spikey hair, a choker-type necklace on and funky clothes talking on the phone. As I get closer she actually turns her back to me.

Yes, my blood is starting to boil. I can tell she is talking to her boyfriend. I get to the counter and go around the side so she can see me and put my finger in the air to ask for just one minute. She looks at me in disgust and puts the phone to her shoulder and says, "Can I help you?" in her most annoyed voice.

Here was my response in my most excited and energetic voice: "I know you are super-busy, but my husband just called and told me we have tickets to this huge gala dinner event, and I need a gorgeous dress, shoes, a purse, everything. I bet you know the store in and out, and I was just thinking it would be a blast if you could help me get in and out of here in the next 30 minutes and help me look awesome for this gala event! Is there any way you would help me?"

She puts the phone to her ear, says, "I gotta go," hangs up and says, "OH, this is gonna be so much fun. Sure, I'll help you. Let's go!"

We were done in 30 minutes, everything paid for. Jessica even called ahead to the valet for my car and walked me to the front door! She hugged me as I left, and said, "That was the best 30 minutes I have ever had working here!" I sent her a thank you card and contacted her supervisor to tell her about the fantastic experience I had with Jessica.

So how did Dawn utilize serving others in the above scenario? Well, could you imagine if Dawn had gone to the counter and began tapping her nails on the counter to get the gal's attention? What if she said "You need to help me, I need a dress, and I have to be out of here in 30 minutes!"? Maybe a little too demanding.

By understanding Jessica's behavioral style, Dawn was simply able to speak her language, treat her appropriately and have her feel amazing about the whole situation. Just because Dawn served Jessica, Jessica had a memorable experience and by her words, her favorite 30 minute experience of ever working at Macy's.

What if by knowing this information your goal could be to leave people better than you found them? You tend to hear that phrase when talking about a place or location like a camp site. Leave it better than you found it. Could you do that with people?

You can really serve someone else by making their day and putting them first. Try it! It is rewarding, fun, easy and you get to bring out the best in others and yourself! When you choose to serve others with this material, we can promise that your life will change in direct proportion with how freely you serve them.

Okay, are you looking for more concrete tools? We want to make it very clear that your mindset, your awareness, your intentions and your ability to serve others ARE going to be your biggest and best tools. But we do have some more *how-to* type of tools for you as well.

Platinum Rule® Assessment

Your own personal Platinum Rule® Assessment is the next best tool you could ever have. Not only does it give you documented, credible information about your own behavioral style, you can also choose to have up to 100 other people assess you and see where their perception of you falls onto the graph.

This can be incredibly eye opening. See, other people might see you differently than you see yourself. Knowing which style your family, co-workers, or friends view you as can help you determine the quality of the relationships. Tony calls this part of the Platinum Rule® Assessment the 360-degree view. It is a full 360-degree view of how others perceive you.

Are you unconsciously adapting in certain situations, and you don't even know it? Because of certain pressures, bosses, or simply a task you are required to do at work – do people view you differently than you are?

The 27-page report that you receive is based upon your unique blend of all four styles. There are tens of thousands of combinations available, and this report takes into consideration your unique blend of all four styles. Plus, the last several pages of the report are what we like to call "cheat sheets." They're your super-quick reminder of the how-tos that we were talking about earlier.

If you are a Promoter, would you like to have a quick refresher on how to adapt to a Nurturer? Your report will give that to you. If you are a fast-paced person, would you like to have several options available for you to adapt to slower-paced people? This is all available in the blink of an eye with your report.

In fact, many of our clients take the last several pages, laminate them and keep them in a notebook that is with them at all times. That way as they are about to go into a meeting with a newly-referred prospect, they can remind themselves of how that person should be worked with.

Then there are more specific referral processes that we know you'll want more information on. For example, would you like to know how to talk to a prospect that needs to be referred to someone in your referral network? Would you like to understand the ways that you would want to adapt to that person's style and actually have them be compelled to be referred to you versus pressuring them to be referred to you?

Note, the first version of the sentence above sounded like this: Would it be powerful to know the decisive techniques that you need to adapt to that person's style and actually make them compelled to be referred versus pressured to be referred?

Can you hear all of the Go-Getter words in there? Does it sound more demanding than the second sentence? Remember, we always bring our own style to the table first. If you want to appeal to more of the population, then you have to speak their language too!

If at the beginning of the book, you chose not to purchase the Platinum Rule® Assessment, we understand. But after reading and learning this information, we hope that you see the incredible value in truly understanding you first! It is only when you understand yourself to the fullest degree does seeing others become second nature. We encourage you to get the assessment now. All you need to do is go to www.RoomFullofReferrals.com.

We would also like you to get some other very important documents that will help you with this material. Here are just a few of the items that are available at www.RoomFullofReferrals.com under the Free Downloads:

- Excel Referral Institute Tracking & Rewarding
- Establishing Referral Relationships
- How to Adapt to Referral Sources
- Videos by Dawn Lyons and Dr. Tony Alessandra
- And much more!

CHAPTER 15

Creating Long-Term Referral Relationships

Life is funny sometimes. When you look back and think about all of the people who have come into life and out of your life over the years, it's pretty amazing. The different behavioral styles with different strengths, lessons to teach you or simply just different levels of friendship is just mind-blowing.

Knowing what you know now about behavioral styles can you see how in some cases you actually may have been seeking a certain style to help you with something at that moment? Think back to a time when you just really needed someone to listen to you, did you call a Nurturer? What about a time when you needed something taken care immediately and couldn't do it yourself? Maybe you contacted a Go-Getter or Examiner. What about the days when you just needed to let loose and have some fun. Did you connect with a Promoter?

See, life *is* funny. You have all of these different types of people in your life to help you in so many ways. Yet, how often does it happen that you get bored, annoyed, impatient or frustrated with them? The reality is *they* have strengths and challenges, too! We believe that if more individuals had a better understanding of people, then they could easily respect the strengths and challenges of the people around them and utilize their best qualities.

We want you to do another exercise. This is a very important process in thoroughly owning this material and truly understanding the depth of people and how you interact with them. This exercise could prove to be a turning point in how you treat others, work with them, view them and respect them. If you have not done any of the other exercises, PLEASE do this one!

The exercise is called "from reality to respect." We would like you to write down five things or characteristics about each one of the behavioral styles that annoys you. For example, maybe the Examiners ask too many questions, or you feel the Nurturers are overly sensitive. Maybe the Promoters are too excitable,, and the Go-Getters are just too demanding.

Whatever your annoyances are with each style, write them down below. Yes, you'll write about your own style as well! This is your current reality of each of the styles

What Annoys You about Each Style

Please list the five things that frustrate you or annoy you about each style now.

Go-Getters

1.____

2.____

3.____

4.____

5.____

Promoters

1.____

2.____

3.____

4.____

5.____

Nurturers

1.____

2.____

3.____

4.____

5.____

Examiners

1.____

2.____

3.____

4.____

5.____

The next step of this exercise is to write down, with the knowledge you have learned about each of the styles, a reason why you now respect that quality in them. Yes, respect it!

For example…

> *Examiners ask too many questions. I respect that because I realize they are trying to gather enough information to make a decision.*
>
> *Nurturers are too overly sensitive. I respect that because I realize the depth with which they care for people.*
>
> *Promoters are too excited. I respect that because they're simply having fun and sharing their excitement.*
>
> *Go-Getters are too demanding. I respect that because they're just trying to get the right result.*

Here is the key. Developing a true reason as to why you can respect each style's "annoying" traits is crucial. Again, the more you honor others for their strengths, the less you will be annoyed or frustrated. Use the space below to fill in your answers.

We highly recommend you read these out loud after you have done each style. It will help engage your mind and have a longer-lasting effect. For those that are a bit harder for you to find a reason to respect… you may have to read them over and over again! Remember, it is a process.

Go-Getters

Please fill in your answer from above then complete the statement.

1.___________________________________, I respect that because

2.___________________________________, I respect that because

3.___________________________________, I respect that because

4.___________________________________, I respect that because

5.___________________________________, I respect that because

Promoters

Please fill in your answer from above then complete the statement.

1.____________________________________, I respect that because

____

____

____

2.____________________________________, I respect that because

____

____

____

3.____________________________________, I respect that because

____

____

____

4.____________________________________, I respect that because

____

____

____

5.____________________________________, I respect that because

____

____

____

Nurturers

Please fill in your answer from above then complete the statement.

1.____________________________________, I respect that because

____

____

____

2.____________________________________, I respect that because

____

____

____

3.____________________________________, I respect that because

____

____

____

4.____________________________________, I respect that because

____

____

____

5.____________________________________, I respect that because

____

____

____

Examiners

Please fill in your answer from above then complete the statement.

1.______________________________________, I respect that because

____

____

____

2.______________________________________, I respect that because

____

____

____

3.______________________________________, I respect that because

____

____

____

4.______________________________________, I respect that because

____

____

____

5.______________________________________, I respect that because

____

____

____

How did that feel? Did you actually take the time to do the exercise (Go-Getters and Promoters, I'm talking to you)? Did your reasons for respecting them seem truthful? Did you find yourself having a deeper respect for each of the styles? Was it hard to come up with a way to respect a particular characteristic?

Remember, part of understanding people is understanding why you might be annoyed with them. Respecting other people is respecting how they are hard-wired. These characteristics are something that is so ingrained in them they don't even recognize it.

Typically, each style can come up with the top characteristics that envelope that style. But interestingly, they also believe that other people see them that way. How about a list of how each style views themselves and another list of how others might view them? Would that help?

Go-Getters

You see yourselves as:	*Others may view you as:*
Confident	Arrogant
Bold	Selfish
Determined	Rude
Decisive	Demanding
Goal-Oriented	Impatient
Strong	Domineering
Ambitious	

Continue on next page

Promoters

You see yourselves as:	*Others may view you as:*
Positive	Flighty
Imaginative	Frivolous
Enthusiastic	Distracted
Optimistic	Lacking in determination
Fun-loving	Lacking in focus
Gregarious	Shallow
Spontaneous	Loud
	Party animals

Nurturers

You see yourselves as:	*Others may view you as:*
Caring	Needy
Helpful	Boring
Stable	Timid
Sincere	Easy mark
Patient	Worrisome
Kind	Sappy
Great listeners	Slow
	Spineless

Examiners

You see yourselves as:	*Others may view you as:*
Calculating	Picky
Detailed	Harsh
Solitary	Strict
Observant	Finicky
Efficient	Uncaring
Effective	Superior
Perfectionist	Emotionless

Knowing how each style is hard-wired, can you see how important it is to be able to adapt to others? We certainly hope so! It will take you much, much further in your relationships. In fact, let's see how much you have learned from reading this book. Remember the assessment you took at the beginning? Let's look at that again and see if your point total has changed.

Referral Marketing Assessment Using Behavioral Styles

- I understand the strengths and weaknesses of all four behavioral styles.

Lowest 0 1 2 3 4 5 *Highest*

- I understand how my own style is affecting my referability.

Lowest 0 1 2 3 4 5 *Highest*

- I can identify the styles of my top 10 referral sources.

Lowest 0 1 2 3 4 5 *Highest*

- When at networking functions, I can observe the four different styles.

Lowest 0 1 2 3 4 5 *Highest*

- When I meet someone, I can identify his or her top two styles within 20-30 seconds.

Lowest 0 1 2 3 4 5 *Highest*

- I understand the language of all four styles.

Lowest 0 1 2 3 4 5 *Highest*

- When I meet someone, I can immediately begin to speak to them in their language.

Lowest 0 1 2 3 4 5 *Highest*

- When I meet someone, I am able to change my pace, hand gestures and tonality.

Lowest 0 1 2 3 4 5 *Highest*

- When I meet someone, I am able to manage the conversation so that they appreciate the conversation.

Lowest 0 1 2 3 4 5 *Highest*

Continue on next page

- When working with referral sources, I always adapt to their style.

Lowest 0 1 2 3 4 5 Highest

- When working with referral sources, I am aware of how they want to be trained by style.

Lowest 0 1 2 3 4 5 Highest

- When working with referral sources, I follow up with them based on their behavioral style.

Lowest 0 1 2 3 4 5 Highest

- When working with referral sources, I am able to have them teach me what style their referred prospect is before I meet with them.

Lowest 0 1 2 3 4 5 Highest

- When working with referral sources, I always reward them based on their behavioral style.

Lowest 0 1 2 3 4 5 Highest

- When working with referral sources, I am always aware of their style and how to serve them as we work together.

Lowest 0 1 2 3 4 5 Highest

Next, please add up your points: ______
Did you rate higher this time? Has your awareness increased? Did your number of points increase? Did you hit a different level even?

If so, fantastic, you are really getting it! If not, remember, it is a process. Especially if this is your first time engaging in this type of material, keep learning. There are many resources out there.

Check to see if the Referral Institute is in your area at www.referralinstitute.com and click on Regional Headquarters.

You can also pick up other books written by Tony at amazon.com, including *The Platinum Rule® for DiSC® Sales Mastery* by Tony Alessandra and Scott Zimmerman; *Selling with Style* by Don Hutson, Tony Alessandra and Scott Zimmerman; *The NEW Art of Managing People* by Phil Hunsaker and Tony Alessandra;

The Platinum Rule for Small Business Mastery by Tony Alessandra, Ron Finkelstein and Scott Zimmerman; and P*eople Smart in Business* by Tony Alessandra and Michael O'Connor

Please note he has different titles for each of the behavioral styles in his other books.

Or, you can purchase the Platinum Rule® Assessment so you understand *you* first and have the entire 27-page report to look at and learn from regularly.

"I wanted to share with you the benefit I got from Room Full of Referrals™. I was there with an employee, and I am a Go-Getter, and they are an Examiner. I was feeling a little frustrated because I was expecting the Examiner to do things the way I do them. Big mistake on my part.

"I could tell he was frustrated with how I was communicating to him. After the program I realized that I needed to write things out and send them to him as opposed to calling him and leaving it on his voicemail and expecting it to happen quickly. By having it written out that helps him to help me get things accomplished.

"The Go-Getter in me is satisfied and the Examiner in him can support me in my quest to grow my business. I also found that I can relate to others as well now that I know where they are coming from and what works for them."

Steven Montoya • Computer Solutions of Marin • www.computersolutionsofmarin.com

A Story from Dawn: The Three Words

While working out with my trainer, pro bodybuilder Chris Jantz, one day, he mentioned that he is inspired by three words when training for a competition: simplicity, intensity and consistency. I found that very interesting as it relates fully to what we are asking you to do with this material.

Simplicity

See, Chris says, "Keep it simple, don't over think it, the basics work!" Remember, Ivan's story about the wind sprints? You have just learned the basics of behavioral styles. Keep going over them, and you will become more proficient at this.

Intensity

Chris talks about crossing the line of intensity to force the body to change. Well, intensity plays a role in behavioral styles in three ways:

1. You have the different degrees of intensities between the four styles in each and every individual in the world.
2. The intensity at which you choose to implement this material will have a direct correlation on how quickly you take your referral relationships to the next level.
3. We hope you have taken your mind across that line of intensity and forced your activities with other people to change based on their behavioral styles.

Consistency

In bodybuilding, it means small, steady steps. It's the same with behavioral styles. Remember unconscious competence? That's what consistency will bring to you when you choose to use this material in all of your daily activities. Very interesting to see how a concept in bodybuilding works in behavioral styles, too!

We would like to ask you, can you keep it simple and focus on the basics, keep up your intensity of learning this material and will you stay consistently aware that your behavioral style is affecting your referability? We certainly hope so! And, you also have the ability to improve your relationships.

If you're like most people, you want to learn more about *why* you do what you do and improve your interactions with others. This book has given you a simple, yet proven, way to do just that! Understanding yourself and your behavioral patterns more thoroughly in order to adapt and treat others the way that they want to be treated is something we can accomplish each and every day. This can only impart a more positive experience with every individual that you encounter.

By mastering the content of this book, our intention is that it will not only help you become an even better you, it will help you to positively influence those around you. With our specific focus on referral marketing and networking, we hope you see that these opportunities are all around you.

Behavioral style is a pattern or a group of recurring habits resulting from the way that you typically do things – even the way you deal with people and situations. It is your comfortable method of behaving when you are just being you.

Often, when you do what comes naturally to you, you alienate others without even realizing it. Why? Well, hopefully you have learned that your behavior may not be what is natural for someone else and different can be challenging.

If we want to truly connect with our colleagues, friends, bosses, family, and, of course, referral sources – then it is imperative that we become aware of our natural tendencies *and* other people's natural preferences! Essentially, you will then be defusing any extreme behaviors before you sabotage yourself and your relationships.

You have learned the skills in this book to be able to simply adapt your language, hand gestures, tonality, etc. to ensure the person you are interacting with is extremely comfortable in the conversation. Use it and enjoy the rewards. Choose not to and you may continue to be consistently frustrated with people!

People all over the world desire strong, deep, personal relationships. It is part of being a human being. Creating those long-term meaningful relationships is 100% up to you. From this book we hope you have gained:

- A better understanding of how you are wired.
- The ability to identify other people's style.
- A strong desire to treat other people the way that they want to be treated.
- A deeper level of knowledge about your strengths and your challenges.
- And the ability to see those strengths and challenges in others too.
- Better information as to where you truly are in your referral marketing efforts in your business.
- Some new ideas on how you can motivate others – with the right intentions!
- Four new languages that you can clearly speak.
- Appropriate ways to gain appointments with new clients and even referral sources.
- A process of proactively wanting to develop and create your own diverse network.
- New insights on how you can train your referral network more thoroughly and in a way that they want to learn in order to gain you more referral business.
- The proper mindset and tools to be able to adapt naturally to others.

And, most of all, we hope you have gained the respect that each behavioral style is needed, necessary, important, powerful, useful, and much, much more! Your referral marketing efforts depend on it!

Remember, from here on, you are completely aware that there are four distinct behavioral styles. As a business owner you may be doing tons of networking in your area, and you are constantly walking into rooms full of people. You are seeking to do more business by referral, and you now know "Referral Marketing... you just can't do it alone" and therefore you need to identify, develop, train and reward your referral network!

Your mindset, now that you understand behavioral styles, is that you are always walking into a Room Full of Referrals™, and how you treat others will determine your success each and every day!

We believe in you! That you WILL truly adopt this new way of living and Create Referrals For Life®!

About the Authors

Dr. Tony Alessandra helps companies and salespeople turn prospects into promoters. He is two speakers in one... a professor and a performer, or as one client put it – he delivers college lectures in a comedy store format.

Dr. Tony offer audiences the opportunity to enjoy themselves while learning practical, immediately applicable skills that positively impact their relationships with prospects, customers and co-workers. His focus is on how to create instant rapport with prospects, employees & vendors; how to convert prospects and customers into business apostles who will "preach the gospel" about your company and products; and how to out-market, out-sell and out-service the competition.

Dr. Alessandra has a street-wise, college-smart perspective on business, having been raised in the housing projects of NYC to eventually realizing success as a graduate professor of marketing, Internet entrepreneur, business author, and hall-of-fame keynote speaker. He earned a BBA from the Univ. of Notre Dame, an MBA from the Univ. of Connecticut and his PhD in marketing in 1976 from Georgia State University.

In addition to being president of Assessment Business Center, a company that offers online 360° assessments, Tony is also a founding partner in the Platinum Rule Group — a company which has successfully combined cutting-edge technology and proven psychology to give salespeople the ability to build and maintain positive relationships with hundreds of clients and prospects.

Dr. Alessandra is a prolific author with 27 books translated into over 50 foreign language editions, including the newly revised, bestselling *The NEW Art of Managing People* (Free Press/Simon & Schuster, 2008); *Charisma* (Warner Books, 1998); *The Platinum Rule* (Warner Books, 1996); *Collaborative Selling* (John Wiley & Sons, 1993); and *Communicating at Work* (Fireside/Simon & Schuster, 1993). He is featured in over 50 audio/video programs and films, including Relationship Strategies (American Media); The Dynamics of Effective Listening (Nightingale-Conant); and Non-Manipulative Selling (Walt Disney). He is also the originator of the internationally-recognized behavioral style assessment tool - The Platinum Rule®.

Recognized by *Meetings & Conventions Magazine* as *"one of America's most electrifying speakers,"* Dr. Alessandra was inducted into the Speakers Hall of Fame in 1985. In 2009, he was inducted as one of the "Legends of the Speaking Profession;" in 2010, 2011 & 2012, he was selected as one of the Top 5 Marketing Speakers by Speaking.com; in 2010, Tony was elected into the inaugural class of the Sales Hall of Fame; in 2012, he was voted one of the Top 50 Sales & Marketing Influencers; and also in 2012, Dr. Tony was voted the #1 World's Top Communication Guru. Tony's polished style, powerful message, and proven ability as a consummate business strategist consistently earn rave reviews and loyal clients.

Contact information for Dr. Tony Alessandra

Keynote Speeches: Holli Catchpole
Phone: 1-760-603-8110
Email: Holli@SpeakersOffice.com

Corporate Training or Cyrano CRM System: Scott Zimmerman
Phone: 1-330-848-0444 x2
Email: Scott(at)PlatinumRule.com

Online Assessments: Brandon Parker
Phone: 1-760-872-1500
Email: BParker@Assessments.ws

About the Authors

Dr. Ivan Misner is the founder and chairman of BNI, the world's largest business networking organization. BNI was founded in 1985. The organization has almost 6,200 chapters throughout every populated continent of the world. Last year alone, BNI generated 6.9 million referrals resulting in $3.1 billion dollars' worth of business for its members.

Dr. Misner's Ph.D. is from the University of Southern California. He is a *New York Times* bestselling author who has written 16 books including his latest #1 best seller about "gender," *Business Networking and Sex (not what you think)*.

He is a monthly columnist for Entrepreneur.com and Fox Business News and has taught business management at several universities throughout the United States. In addition, he is the Senior Partner for the Referral Institute - a referral training company with trainers around the world.

Called the *"Father of Modern Networking"* by CNN and the *"Networking Guru"* by Entrepreneur magazine, Dr. Misner is considered one of the world's leading experts on business networking and has been a keynote speaker for major corporations and associations throughout the world. He has been featured in the *L.A. Times, Wall Street Journal, and New York Times*, as well as numerous TV and radio shows including *CNN, CNBC, the BBC and The Today Show on NBC.*

Dr. Misner is on the Board of Trustees for the University of La Verne. He is also the Founder of the BNI-Misner Foundation and was recently named "Humanitarian of the Year" by the Red Cross. He is married and lives with his wife Elisabeth and their three children in Claremont, California. In his spare time!!! he is also an amateur magician and a black belt in karate.

In the early 1980s, he started a management consulting practice in Southern California. The one issue that kept coming up over and over again was: "How do you manage and motivate employees?" What he learned during this period was that you "can't" motivate people. The truth is that they have to motivate themselves. The best a business owner can do is to provide an environment that is conducive to creating motivation within someone.

The question then was – "how do you do that?" Ivan believed the answer was in the realm of understanding the employee better. And the most effective way to do that was to get a sense of what their behavioral styles were. So he went through a 40+ hour certification program by the J.P. Cleaver company to learn their behavioral system and used that system as the basis of his work with many companies for the next decade.

To contact Dr. Ivan Misner, visit www.IvanMisner.com

About the Authors

Dawn Lyons has spent over 24+ years learning, understanding and applying behavioral styles into her life. It was in December of 1988 that Dawn was exposed to a seminar that gave a very short description about the different behavioral styles. Realizing at 18 years old how important this information could be, she set out to master the material.

In fact, Dawn has been hired to speak in Ireland, Germany, UK, Australia, Sweden and all across the US to audiences of 500+. Dawn is a contributing author to the *New York Times* bestselling book, *Masters of Sales*, in which she describes how to use behavioral styles to sell to people appropriately.

Dawn became a BNI franchise owner in 2000 and began working with business owners and entrepreneurs. In May of 2004, Ivan referred her to the Referral Institute to become a franchise owner in the San Francisco Bay Area. In November of 2004, she was the keynote presenter at the BNI International Conference with over 500+ people from over 20 different countries.

It was after Dawn completed the keynote presentation that she went to Mike Macedonio, the president of Referral Institute, and suggested that a behavioral styles training program be offered. Being a certified DiSC® trainer, Dawn personally created a three and a half hour program called Room Full of Referrals®, which is 100% focused on how your behavioral style is affecting your referability. Room Full of Referrals® is currently being taught in 13 different countries to thousands of business owners.

This book has been derived from this program and is a perfect beginning to learning about behavioral styles or the perfect follow up after taking Room Full of Referrals® in your area. In 2006, Dawn became a vice president and partner with Referral Institute. With over 24 years of experience and training thousands of participants, Dawn's expertise lies in being able to identify the different styles and immediately adapt pace of speech, eye contact, posture, hand gestures and even language.

Dawn also owns two franchises of Referral Institute in the San Francisco Bay Area where she is dedicated to training local business owners in all of the seminars that Referral Institute offers, along with personal consulting.

Her passion however does lie in the Room Full of Referrals® program as she believes that more people must understand that their behavioral style is affecting their referability for the good and the not so good! Her desire is to have people truly become masters at this material.

For corporate training, keynote presentations or personal consulting, email office@referralinstitute.com or call 707-780-8110

REFERRAL® INSTITUTE

The Referral Institute provides the training and tools to help business professionals gain financial success through relationship-based referral marketing. Our "Referrals for Life®" program is not a numbers game - it is not about spending hours making cold calls, collecting business cards, or developing a huge database of prospective customers. We don't want you to work harder to gain new business - we want you to learn how to work smarter. With the Referrals for Life® program, business referrals do not happen by accident. They result from implementing, and then consistently monitoring, a well-organized referral marketing plan.

The Referral Institute is an international franchised referral training and consulting company with locations in Australia, the Middle East, Europe, and North America. At The Referral Institute, we'll teach you how to make all your business relationships become more valuable to you and your business. As a result, you'll not only enjoy an increased quality of life because your business is flourishing, but you will also gain lifelong relationships: Referrals for Life®.

If you are a motivated business professional serious about moving your business to the next level, don't wait to contact the Referral Institute headquarters nearest to you.

Please go to www.referralinstitute.com to learn more about referral marketing, as well as how to attend a Referral Institute training program in your area. You may contact the organization at: info@referralinstitute.com to talk about growing your business by generating qualified referrals.

BNI®

BNI, the world's largest business networking organization, was founded by Dr. Ivan Misner in 1985 as a way for businesspeople to generate referrals in a structured, professional environment. The organization, now the world's largest referral business network, has thousands of chapters with tens of thousands of members on every populated continent. Since its inception, BNI members have passed millions of referrals, generating billions of dollars in business for the participants.

The primary purpose of the organization is to pass qualified business referrals to its members. The philosophy of BNI may be summed up in two simple words: Givers Gain®. If you give business to people, you will get business from them. BNI allows only one person per profession to join a chapter. The program is designed to help businesspeople develop long-term relationships, thereby creating a basis for trust and, inevitably, referrals. The mission of BNI is to help members increase their business through a structured, positive, and professional word-of-mouth program that enables them to develop long-term, meaningful relationships with quality business professionals.

To visit a chapter near you, contact BNI via email at: bni@bni.com or visit its website at www.bni.com

NOTES

NOTES

NOTES

NOTES

NOTES

NOTES

NOTES